SEE POVERTY...

Be The Difference!

*Discovering the Missing Pieces
for Helping People Move Out of Poverty*

Dr. Donna Marie Beegle

with
Debbie Ellis
Dr. Rima Akkary

Our Mission:

Communication Across Barriers is dedicated to broadening and improving opportunities for people who live with the trauma inflicted by poverty conditions. Our goals are to:

- Provide life-changing information that shatters common myths and stereotypes about people who live in poverty

- Offer research based strategies for improving relationships, communication, and opportunities for lifelong success for people who live in poverty

Printed October 2006
Copyright © by Donna M. Beegle, Ed.D.
All rights reserved

ISBN-13: 978-1-934085-00-4
ISBN-10: 1-934085-00-6

Discounts on bulk quantities of this book are available. For details and discount information, contact Communication Across Barriers, book@combarriers.com, or visit the web site, www.combarriers.com.

Published in the United States of America by
Communication Across Barriers, Inc.
PO Box 23071
Tigard, OR 97281-3071
www.combarriers.com

Cover design and book layout by Donna's cousin,
Wanda Buck, of Lou Graphics
(www.lougraphics.com)

1980

CONTENTS

List of Activities

ACKNOWLEDGMENTS

For years, I have wanted to compile my work in a usable format to increase awareness and opportunities for people living in poverty. I would still be wishing for that
luxury if not for the incredible team that said, "I can help make this book a reality."
They came together to write, edit, design graphics and activities. I am humbled
by their talents and am in awe of their devotion to making a difference for people
in poverty. A special thank you goes to Debbie Ellis and Rima Akkary, our editors.
Debbie, Rima and I spent so much time going over the content I often felt like we
were "sharing brains". They are brilliant, talented writers, editors and both women
that I consider to be friends. I also want to recognize the efforts of my cousin,
Wanda Buck, who did all layout and graphics for this book. Like me, Wanda, grew
up in abject poverty and lived much of her childhood in a car. Wanda's poverty experiences and graphic talents truly make the cover and the inside of this book come
alive. Each time I would describe what I wanted to convey, Wanda would come
back with a perfect image or graphic to capture it. My eternal gratitude goes to this
team who often worked with no pay and worked in addition to their "real" jobs.
Each person contributed their strengths as much as they could to make this effort a
success. Everyone on the team is committed to ending poverty. Like moving out of
poverty, a project like this does not happen without people helping each other.

Many thanks to the Communication Across Barriers Team:

Dr. Rima Akkary
Richard Ambert
Jenice Artman
Wayne Austin
Wanda Buck
Steve Carlson
Lynda Coates
Debbie Ellis
Chuck Forbes
Dr. Debbie Hornibrook
Allen Koshewa
Gwen McNeir
Jared Moultrie
Dr. Eileen Casey White
Dr. Ed Wilgus

My mom, Ruth Austin, could have been President of the United States. She's resilient, brilliant, a problem solver and never gives up on people. Instead of becoming educated and leading our country, she grew up picking cotton for survival and dropped out of school in eighth grade to help care for her younger siblings after her dad died of cancer. Throughout her life and while raising six children as she continued to cope with poverty, my mom has always considered the well being of others and maintained optimism. Her life motto is, "Tomorrow will be a better day. Let's just work together and get through today."

As I write this dedication page for my first book, *See Poverty…Be the Difference,* my 70 year-old mom lies in recovery from double bi-pass heart surgery. The surgery was a success, but there are complications. She has one kidney, lupus, chronic bronchitis, arthritis, and has recently had a stroke. Her body and her health complications are directly derived from a lifetime of poverty without proper nutrition or health care and the daily stress that comes from not having your basic needs met. As I leaned over to give her a hug before her surgery, my tears fell. My mom was heavily sedated and her hands tied down to prevent her from pulling at the wires and tubes hooked up to her body. I cried, "Mom, I am not ready to lose you. I do not know enough." My mom rose up and opened one eye as if trying to hug and reassure me. Even severely ill, I knew, she is still taking care of me.

This book is dedicated to my mom. She has spent her life making life better for everyone she comes into contact with. A smile, a compliment, a blanket, a bowl of beans, some wisdom—she did not have much, but she always gave. My mom taught me that I was special, but not better than anyone else. She taught me that people are the most important thing in the world and that if you can help, you should. She cared for my children while I was in school and gave me constant encouragement to complete my education. Without my mom, there would be no book.

INTRODUCTION

My education, my work, and my passion are to help people from all races who are trapped in poverty. I want them to have genuine options for lifelong success. This can only happen if the voices of those struggling with poverty can be heard and their perspectives understood.

For more than one hundred years, gender and race have dominated discussions of diversity. When class or issues of poverty enter the conversation, it is generally assumed that people are making choices that determine their "lot" in life. This myth of choice continues even with astounding evidence that children born into poverty in the Unites States (regardless of their race and gender) face dramatically different futures than children born to affluence. Their chances of continuing to be as poorly endowed as their parents are great in spite of hard work. As the gap increases between those who are educated and those who are not—between those who are "making it" and those who are not—so grows the gap in our awareness that poverty is a diversity issue. We cannot remain silent.

People from poverty are isolated and have few opportunities to interact with others who are not in situations like them. When they do have interactions outside their own group, it is most often with four kinds of helping professionals: educators, social service providers, health care workers, and police officers and other law enforcement officials. Universities train these helping professionals to maintain their distance from the people with whom they work. Organizations set policies such as: "Don't get personal." "Do not share personal stories." "Maintain professionalism." These teachings prevent people from connecting in ways that can break the cycle of poverty.

There is little training or education about poverty in the United States; what we learn about poverty is generally from the media. Helping professionals are left on their own to discover how to effectively educate, communicate, and work with those they are trying to serve. It is the goal of this book to help create an understanding of poverty and to promote the development of meaningful ways to help people have genuine opportunities for getting out of poverty and finding pathways to lifelong success.

Most of the research on poverty is conducted by people who have never experienced generational poverty. It is the outsider looking in and often interpreting meaning and behavior without considering the social class context. While, you do not have to "live" poverty to understand it, it is easy when looking in from a different class perspective to misunderstand and judge the behavior from what a middle-class person would do in a similar situation. For example, in the literature review for my doctoral dissertation, I reviewed hundreds of studies that indicated parents in poverty did not "support" their children's education. The researchers often defined "support" as getting the kids to school on time, showing up for conferences, being involved in school activities, and creating a time and a place for homework. When these behaviors did not happen, the data were interpreted as the parents not supporting their child's education. The reality is that when you are living in the crisis of poverty, it is difficult to do anything but respond to the crisis needs. My parents never went to a school conference. I never knew an adult who did. My mom would say, "I ain't going in there and make a fool of myself. Those people want to talk about school. I don't know anything about school." But as you read my story on the following pages, you will see all the ways that my family supported me from the GED to my doctorate.

Another example of an outsider looking in and misinterpreting behavior is reflected in statements that report that the reason students from poverty do not respect their teachers is that they have no adults in their lives worthy of respect.

Looking in at my mom from a middle-class framework, you might see a woman who wrote bad checks and sold her food stamps. Looking at my dad, you might see a man who drinks Mad Dog wine and smokes Pall Mall cigarettes. Looking at my parents from living in poverty, I saw my mom as the one who could get food on the table and keep our heat on when all the money was gone. The bad checks were for groceries—selling food stamps was to pay our electric bill. My dad was not born an alcoholic. He became one after years of working 16 hours a day, being paid very little cash, and saying to my mom, "Ruth, should I give all this money to the landlord or do you want me to keep a little back for groceries?" Cigarettes were a way to calm his nerves in the war zone of poverty that we lived in. He eventually became an alcoholic to escape the pain of living in a social system that sent strong messages that, as a man, he was a failure because he could not take care of his family. I saw my dad as funny, intelligent, strong and so talented. He could pick a 12 string guitar like no one I have ever met.

I do not proclaim to have all the answers or insights for solving the problems of poverty. However, I do assert that having lived essentially homeless for 28 years of my life, I present a unique insider perspective.

See Poverty…Be the Difference is a weaving of my personal experiences of growing up in generational poverty with seventeen years of work and research on that topic, including sharing the voices of others who have broken the barriers of poverty to find educational and lifelong success. I share these stories, not as "shining" examples of how individuals can succeed, but as proof of the possibilities available—and those that can be made available—to make success part of the story of every person trapped in poverty. I offer them to you as examples of "everyone's story" who has ever grown up in poverty. To me, meanings of words are shaped by life experiences and the context in which people live.

It is also my hope that reading these stories will help you reflect on your own story. How did you come to be where you are in life? What are your own attitudes, beliefs, and values toward poverty and the people who are experiencing it? Your own reflection can bring you closer to the struggles that people in poverty endure—thus illuminating opportunities for shattering some of the barriers that keep them trapped in poverty. The voices are presented here to begin the discussions, so that we all may learn from each other's lived experiences. We have been silent on these issues far too long. Martin Luther King Jr. once said, "Silence about racism perpetuates racism." Silence about poverty will also perpetuate poverty.

See Poverty…Be the Difference provides a foundation for dialogue and action—grounded in research—for impacting the following areas:

AWARENESS AND UNDERSTANDING

- Poverty is a real issue in our society that we have been silent about for far too long.

- The root causes of poverty are structural and embedded in the way we run our organizations and society.

- The differences in life experiences of the various social classes are real and play a crucial role in determining their prospects for success.

- The context of poverty teaches people a unique world-view with its own strengths and challenges.

- Myths and stereotypes about people living in poverty are prevalent in our society.

- Issues of race, class and poverty are closely intertwined; yet they require careful analysis to separate their effects on people's opportunities for success.

- Poverty in the United States is often internalized as a personal deficiency.

- There are characteristics and strengths that exist in the context of poverty.

SERVING

- People living in poverty can—like everybody else—realize big dreams, achieve, and strive for excellence.

- The silence about poverty needs to be broken in order to bring visibility to the struggle of those in poverty.

- Improving communication and adapting to different learning styles are key to enhancing success for people in poverty.

- Effective communication with people from poverty is the main vehicle to hear their voices and honor their worldviews as we plan on how to serve them.

- Mentoring plays a major role in reaching out to and supporting people in poverty.

- Effective help is a collaborative effort requiring partnerships and support systems—not an individual endeavor.

SOCIAL CHANGE

- The structure, culture, and practices within our organizations need to be changed to make them more responsive and better equipped to serve people from poverty.

- The goal is to move beyond helping people cope with poverty and toward providing genuine opportunities for them to achieve and be valued.

- Discovering the issues and questions to consider, as a society, to help eradicate generational poverty is long overdue.

Reading the information in *See Poverty...Be the Difference* may be the first time some of you have had a chance to think about how you have developed your beliefs about and attitudes toward poverty issues. The history and structural causes of poverty in the United States are rarely understood and seldom taught. I applaud your open-mindedness and willingness to take the first step by focusing on poverty and learning new perspectives. For those of you who have thought about it and struggled with the challenges of learning about poverty in the past, I offer you some language and research you may need to talk about these issues with others in similar situations. This book also provides pointers on ways to challenge assumptions, broaden perspectives, question dominant paradigms, or foster change from an insider's perspective.

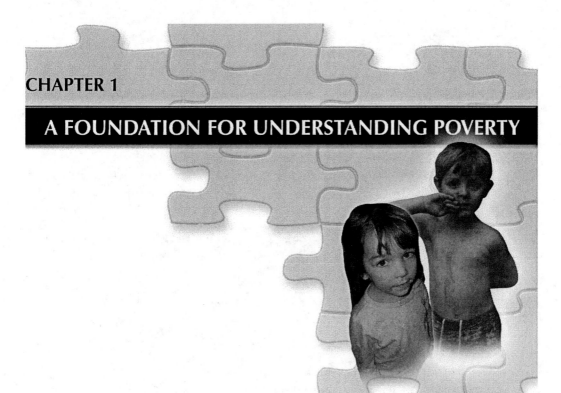

CHAPTER 1

A FOUNDATION FOR UNDERSTANDING POVERTY

THE BLACK HOLE OF POVERTY

by Wayne Austin

THE WEALTHY—Culturally capitalistically; purchased a new reality; luxurious; elementally equal to their environment; paradoxically they care, but are too far removed from the problem

THE SECURE—What is the truth/the nature of truth; can conceive of the problem; possess the level of education needed; not enough of them, not enough resources

THE SAFE—Unable to conceive of the edge; oblivious to the point of poverty; selective reality; too busy for the poor

THE STABLE—There, but for the grace of God; too close to the problem; bootstraps mentality

THOSE ON THE EDGE OF POVERTY

Full of fear; existence is an hourglass; unstable; questionable future

THOSE IN THE BLACK HOLE OF POVERTY

THE FACES OF POVERTY

Misery, hunger, shame; homelessness; hopelessness; being worthless;
the butt of inhumanity; desperation; depression;
destitution; emotional psychosis; manic as a drowning person;
narcoticization; numbness physically, mentally and emotionally;
oblivious to the elements

DEATH THROUGH IMPOVERISHMENT

Note: This piece was written by Dr. Beegle's brother who has spent all of his life in poverty and often in prison. Wayne is currently working on a Master's Degree at Marylhurst University in Portland, Oregon. His passion is in seeking an end to homelessness and poverty for all.

An Insider's Perspective: The Donna Beegle Story

For generations, my family has subsisted on minimum wage employment and migrant work. We have never been landowners—always workers of the land. My grandparents and parents were cotton pickers. My family members were predominantly migrant workers who followed the fruit seasons—picking cherries, berries, potatoes, grapefruit, oranges, beans, and just about anything else that grew. Sometimes we would go into the woods and pull moss or bark off the trees and gather pinecones and mushrooms. We did work that didn't require an education or more skilled labor; jobs that did not ask for references or home telephone numbers. Although we worked hard in migrant labor work and temporary minimum wage jobs, we were constantly being evicted, going hungry, and struggling with poverty.

Donna and brother Steve

I was born into a family where no one was educated beyond the 8th grade. My early experiences in impoverished schools shaped my views and my expectations for my future. In my world, education served as a distraction from being able to meet our daily basic needs or from being close to my family, the only thing I had. I

learned early on that education meant additional "stress" to our family. The stress of trying to arrive on time; having the right clothing, shoes, lunch, and materials for homework projects—all these stresses created a perception that education was not for people like me. I remember silently crying when teachers did not protect me from teasing and ridicule over my ragged clothes, shoes, and lack of middle-class knowledge. These early educational experiences evoke memories of violence, humiliation, and the fear of not fitting in.

Jerry and Donna's wedding

At 12 years old, I met Jerry (also from generational poverty) and, at 15 years old, I dropped out of school to get married. When I told my teacher I was planning to drop out, she told me, "Don't drop out. Some day you may want to get a job." The incentive she was providing to keep me in school—"a job"—had no meaning in the world I came from. To me, meanings were in people, shaped by the context in which they lived. A "job" to me meant working long hours, not being respected, offering little or no hope for moving up, and being paid a below-subsistence wage. I had learned that the American belief that "if you work hard, you'll move up" was a myth for those without education or training. I lived the experience that even though you work long and hard, you rarely move up, you still get evicted, and you often go hungry.

When we married, Jerry was 17 years old and had only a 7th grade education from impoverished schools. He could read and write at about a second-grade level. Jerry and I both began working full-time for minimum wage at a foam rubber factory, but I had to lie about my age since it was illegal to hire a 15-year-old. We moved into a tiny, condemned one-bedroom house in a neighborhood rampant with poverty.

THE PROMISE OF MOTHERHOOD

My dream for as long as I could remember was to be a mom. If my teacher had known me better, she would have known the way to motivate me would have been through my desire to be a mother and be able to provide a good life for my family! I grew up with role models who dropped out of school very young. Every female I ever identified with got married very young and had babies. I did not know anyone who had done anything else, so I was going to do that too. Thus, it is no surprise that my goal in life was to be a mom. For me, having children meant that I would love them, play with them, and that somehow we would find a way to get by and be happy!

I got pregnant right after turning 17. During my pregnancy, I rarely saw a doctor or had anyone to talk to about the upcoming birth. My first baby, Joyce Marie, was born with a head full of black hair and dark blue eyes. She weighed one pound, nine ounces and was eight and a half inches long. She only lived for nine hours, since her lungs were just too tiny to survive. I was devastated by her death. Since I had no camera and no way to get one, I have no pictures of Joyce. All I have to show she even existed is a tiny hospital bracelet and a birth certificate showing her tiny footprint that was the size of the tip of my little finger.

Joyce's bracelet and Infant Admission Information

By now, I was 18 and Jerry was 21. We moved to an impoverished community with my mom, invalid dad, grandmother, uncle, brother Melvin, his wife Mary, their two daughters, and my brothers Wayne and Steve. The 12 of us moved into a house that had no windows and was boarded up. It only had two bedrooms, so Jerry and I slept in the laundry room. Many of us slept on the floor.

Donna pregnant at 18

My 18 year-old solution to the heartbreak of losing my daughter was to get pregnant as fast as possible so I could fulfill my dream. As with my first pregnancy, prenatal care was not part of my life. Welfare policy would not allow me to receive benefits if Jerry was in the home. So, when it got closer to the birth, I lied to my welfare caseworker. I told him that Jerry had left me so I could get a medical card in my fourth month of pregnancy.

On March 23, 1979, Jennifer Marie was born prematurely. She was immediately put on a respirator and an IV inserted into her stomach. When she was 11 days old, the doctors said she had a hole in her heart and needed heart surgery right away. At this point, she weighed only four pounds. They told me she would have a 50 percent chance of surviving the surgery and, if she lived, she would likely suffer from blindness and/or mental challenges from all they were doing to keep her alive. My mom gave me some of her prescribed tranquilizers the day of the surgery. I only remember sitting outside the surgery room crying. I was convinced she would die just like her sister Joyce.

Jennifer survived the heart surgery and was kept on a respirator for two months. Every day, I would sit and rub her skin. I could not hold her, she had too many wires and stitches. She was a beautiful baby with long dark hair and blue eyes. The nurses moved the IV to her head and each day they shaved a little of her hair to accommodate the IV. She could not make a sound because of the respirator in her throat. She would open her mouth to cry, but nothing came out. I cried for her. Deep sobs racked my body. I was terrified of losing my reason for being.

After two and a half months, the doctors told me she weighed five pounds and I could finally take her home. The University of Oregon Health Sciences Center regularly followed the progress of preemie babies, so they did a free check up on Jennifer every six months. Her only lingering problem from her premature birth was that she developed asthma.

Jennifer premature

Jennifer Beegle at Head Start

Since she was considered high risk, Jennifer was placed on top of the waiting list for Head Start, an education program for children in poverty. By this time, I had lost another baby and was pregnant with my son, Danny. Jennifer's teacher, Ms. Susan Proppe-Tong, made every effort to link our family to resources. She told me about the Women, Infant, Children (WIC) nutrition program, and I was able to get juice and milk and healthy foods. I am convinced that it is due to these resources that my son Danny was born healthy and weighed almost six pounds.

Because of my own experiences, I had no trust for educators and was suspicious of Jennifer's teacher even though she had done so much for us. She consistently went out of her way to connect with me. When I arrived to drop Jennifer off or to pick her up, Susan made sure to notice me and to brag on Jennifer (when someone brags on your child enough, you have to like them!). She established some trust by connecting me to resources I was desperate for and, as I gained trust, I confided our family needs. She showed me—and told me—in every way that she loved my little girl, thus I began to feel safe and view her as a partner in getting Jennifer's needs met. I was able to hear her ideas about how I could help Jennifer learn. She even taught me what questions to ask to help Jennifer in elementary school. (I did not even know I could ask questions of school people. I thought we had to take whatever we got. That was what the world of poverty had taught me.) One of the questions Susan told me to ask was about having Jennifer tested for the Talented and Gifted program. I did and Jennifer got in. She had that extra education support all through elementary school and was placed into honors in middle school.

Danny born healthy

THE REALITY OF POVERTY

By the age of 22, I had been through four pregnancies and had two living children. We still had no health care and suffered from poor nutrition. Many nights our dinner was a spoon of peanut butter. During those years, we subsisted on low-wage jobs or welfare—working in migrant labor, pizza parlors, retail, and manufacturing. We moved from place to place hoping for a better life.

My marriage ended in 1986 after 10 years. When Jerry and I split up, my functionally illiterate ex-husband was living in a car that we had bought for $25 at an auction. Unfortunately for Jerry and men like him, there are few, if any, programs for males in poverty in the United States.

Jerry fixes a car bought at an auction

I was now alone trying to care for my six-year-old daughter (who was in the first grade) and two-year-old son. It was not long before we too were evicted and homeless. The difference for me and my children was that we could apply for welfare. We were given $408 per month plus minimal food stamps. With rent at $395, I had just $13 dollars left each month for transportation, clothing, utilities, the Laundromat, soap, shampoo, and other basic necessities. I was constantly making impossible choices…pay the rent or pay the bills…have my utilities shut off or get evicted. My welfare worker told me I needed money management classes so I could stop being evicted. The message to me was clear: "Donna, you are doing something wrong. You need to get it together, work harder. Do something!" But I did work hard. And guess what? None of the minimum wage jobs provided me with a living wage for my little family. All work did for me was take me away from Jennifer and Daniel, my kids, who were my reason for being.

BEGINNING MY EDUCATION

When my lights were turned off for non-payment, I went to a Community Action Agency to ask for help. I was told about a pilot program that was connected to Mount Hood Community College (MHCC), near Portland, Oregon. The program, called Women in Transition (WIT), was designed to be a three-week life skills program for displaced homemakers. Its goal was to help single women gain an education or skills to earn a living for their families. I went to the program not thinking it would change anything, but not knowing what else to do. The director had the wisdom to know that it takes more than three weeks to interrupt poverty. She told the class the WIT staff would be there to support us whenever we needed them—even after the classes ended. I used their services for two years and then became a speaker and advocate on their behalf, sharing how much the program had made a difference in my life. Many of the strategies I teach today I learned in this program.

Jennifer and Danny

The four-member program staff began by sharing their own life experiences. I was amazed. I had never heard the life story of a middle-class person before. I had been so isolated that I had only known people from generational poverty. I learned from the WIT staff that many of them had gone to the same school for more than three or four months, something I had never done. I learned that they had never gone hungry, nor been evicted, nor watched family members treated badly or arrested. I came to realize that they were not better than me. They were people just like me who had different opportunities. And conversely, I was someone just like them, but I had fewer opportunities. This was so empowering. If they weren't better than me, then maybe I too could create the kind of life I wanted for me and my children!

The WIT staff took the time to get to know me and to find out what was important to me. They taught me by using examples from my life to illustrate the concepts they were introducing. They also worked hard on improving my self-concept by teaching me that I was somebody, that I was special. They pointed out that I had accomplished amazing things in my years in poverty, and they praised my resource-fulness. They began exposing me to possibilities for a different future than the one that faced me in poverty.

They helped me with my most pressing needs. A crisis that would normally take me weeks to deal with, they handled in a single phone call. They knew immediately whom to call. They linked me with other programs and built my capacity to have the luxury of learning. I had no idea how much of my brain power and energy were devoted to crisis needs until I began to get some of my needs met.

GETTING MY GED

I came out of the WIT program empowered. I believed I had something to offer, and I had hope. I wrote my dream in my diary: "I want to get a GED (General Equiva-lency Diploma) and maybe someday take a journalism class. Then I will be some-body and be able to take care of Jennifer and Daniel." My motivation and passion throughout the educational journey remained constant. I was motivated by the need and desire to take care of my two children. I wanted to be a good mom, and like all moms, I wanted to be able to care for my children.

My educational journey out of poverty began with my GED. The WIT staff took me to the main campus of MHCC and helped me to establish relationships with faculty, support staff, and resource personnel at the college. They knew that asking me to go on my own would have been too far out of my comfort zone. The WIT staff, along with the staff from the GED program, provided me with a tremendous amount of personal one-on-one teaching. Supported with government

Donna awarded GED

resources to meet my family's basic needs, I was able to reach a milepost and attain my GED.

Graduating with my GED was a huge moment for my family and me. My grand-mother, parents, and brothers all came to the graduation. The ripple effect of my education on my family began shortly after that time, when my brother began work on his GED. I remember thinking that the GED wasn't so bad, that maybe I could get a two-year degree and then I could take even better care of my two children. I had now been exposed to college and to people who were going to college. Once again, I met people who were not that different from me nor better than me—just people with different experiences and opportunities.

OVERCOMING BARRIERS TO EDUCATION

Shortly after my GED graduation, I went to my welfare worker and told her I want-ed to try to get a two-year degree so I would not need government assistance any-more. She quickly told me that the state and federal welfare policies dictate that in order to qualify for welfare I needed to be available for any minimum wage job. If I were in school, I would not be available. If I went to school, the government would sanction me and cut my welfare check from $408 to $258. (This policy is still in effect in all but five states today.) The one thing that kept me from giving up was the "Section-8" public housing certificate from the Portland Housing Authority given to me by the WIT program. (My class was the only group these certificates had been available to within the WIT program; public housing assistance is currently only available to 14 percent of those who qualify.)

As I sat there crying in the welfare office, I began calculating how my kids and I could survive on $258 a month. Not having to worry about being evicted was a huge comfort. I knew I could sell my food stamps for 50 cents per dollar, which would help me pay the utility bills, go to the Laundromat, and buy shampoo and toilet paper. Still, that life was all too familiar to me. I did not know what was ahead, but I knew I did not want to stay in the world of welfare and poverty. I told the welfare worker to "go ahead and cut my check" if that's what she had to do, but I was going to school. My welfare check was reduced to $258, but I still managed to survive by continuing to do many of the survival behaviors that I had done in the past. I went to food banks, clothing closets, and Community Action Agencies.

The WIT staff had connected me with the financial aid office at MHCC. I didn't know someone like me could get money to pay for school. When the community college advisor told me that I could get financial aid to pay for college, I said, "Why don't you pull me up on your fancy-pantsy computer and look at my credit history. Then you won't want to help me at all." I had an attitude. I had a smart mouth. You get that from not having your basic needs met. I was told, "We don't look at credit for financial aid." Astonished, I replied, "Huh? You give people money, and you don't look at their credit?" I didn't live in that world. I lived in a world where I couldn't get anything because I had bad credit. That was my frame of reference.

FURTHERING MY EDUCATION

With an enormous amount of support from the WIT program staff and my family, I entered the community college to work on a two-year degree. I was absolutely terrified. I could not write a complete sentence. The professors wrote words such as "fragment," "double negative," and "run on" on my papers. I did not know what those comments meant,

Jennifer and Donna

but I knew from the red ink that they were bad. I was also baffled by most of the words in the incredibly expensive textbooks. The dictionary was no help; it only gave me more words I did not know. I did not learn what continent I lived on until I was a junior in college. My knowledge gaps were large and served to reinforce my internal feelings that I did not belong in college.

Students from poverty are often placed in special education classes. If they do not know words or concepts, assumptions are made that they are unable to know them—often equating knowing the meaning of a word or subject with intelligence. This happens far too often to children in poverty conditions. But, in fact, if no one around you uses those words or talks about those subjects, a young person is not likely to know the meaning or the subject. Thus my ignorance, much like all students from poverty, had nothing to do with intelligence, but everything to do with growing up in poverty. For instance, I did not have context for subjects such as Watergate. People at the college would often say to me, "How can you not know this? Aren't you American?" They did not understand that while living in poverty, I was in an environment where there was hunger and homelessness; where I was focused on meeting basic needs. Nor did they comprehend that I had attended impoverished schools where the resources were minimal and the teachers were overwhelmed; often an environment that was not conducive to learning.

My language also created difficulties in the education environment. I said, "ain't" every other word. I did not know when it was proper to say "gone" or "went" or "seen" or "saw." I did not know I was not speaking standard English. My only clue was that people judged me as unintelligent. I was rarely asked for my opinions or thoughts and, when I did try to share them, it seemed no one could hear me. I was invisible and, to many people, expendable. I did

Donna and brother Wayne

not look "right," talk "right," or have the "right" family.

An important source of support for getting my two-year degree came from my brother, Wayne. He had spent his last 12 years in prison reading and was amazingly literate. I would write to him and ask about a subject I was studying. He would respond with 25 pages or so using words and examples from our background to explain the subject matter. I could relate to the examples he gave me because they were in our language and were drawn from our life experiences. I rarely read my textbooks; instead I read his letters, and for the most part I did well in my classes.

Letter to Wayne

One day during lunch at MHCC, I stumbled on a college fair. Recruiters from four-year universities were passing out information. A recruiter from the University of Portland asked, "What's your grade point average?" I told him, and he said, "I'll waive the application fee if you would like to apply." My thoughts immediately flew to my kids. Wow, if I could get a four-year degree, I could really take care of Jennifer and Daniel. Because of the location of the University of Portland, I knew I could still rely on my mom and dad to take care of my kids while I attended classes and studied. I could also count on my brothers to help out any way they could. I applied to the University of Portland and received an acceptance letter shortly after. At this time, the primary supports that kept me moving forward in the educational system were the safety of having my housing needs met, the continued support of my family, and having mentors from the WIT program and MHCC who believed in me and encouraged me.

MENTORS, MIDDLE-CLASS LANGUAGE, AND MEETING ME WHERE I WAS–THE KEYS TO MY EDUCATIONAL SUCCESS

My junior year in college I began attending the University of Portland. In one of my first classes there, a professor, Dr. Bob Fulford, asked me if I wanted him to correct my grammar. By this time I had lost my smart mouth and attitude! I said, "Please teach me how to talk like you, because no one thinks I am smart. No one asks my opinion. I feel like no one can hear me." Dr. Fulford was a language specialist and had done extensive work on social-class barriers. He did not tell me to go learn nouns, adjectives, and verbs, as other teachers had done. He knew that what I was doing was, in effect, learning a second language. He knew that people experiencing poverty were often not exposed to the same words or topics that middle-class people talked about. We had a language that related to our poverty experiences. We did not say things incorrectly, but rather in different ways than the middle class said things—consistently speaking with a clear sentence structure and language that did not match what was expected of us in school. He knew that the way for me to learn the meaning of a word was to have someone use it in a context that was familiar to me.

Dr. Fulford began correcting my language every time we spoke. He would stop me at various points in my conversation and say, "Don't say ain't," or "You meant gone, not went." I would chant to myself throughout the day: "Have gone, I went." "I saw, I have seen." After some time, he stopped giving me the correct word. He would simply shake his head no. I would reiterate my point thinking he did not understand, but again he would say, "No." Finally, I would realize my grammar was incorrect and ask for the appropriate wording.

Dr. Fulford also assigned me to read the newspaper. I protested that I did not know the concepts or many of the words used in the articles. It wasn't that I could not understand; it was that in my education, concepts and words were not taught to me in a way that were relevant to my life in poverty. He said I should circle what I did not know or understand and come see him in his office. Then, he would explain—using familiar language and giving examples I could relate to—until I understood it. Dr. Fulford also hired me to grade papers. I now know that he had to grade them again after I had finished them, but the fact that he believed in and trusted me made me try so hard. Because of him, I learned to write. I also learned that the other University students made mistakes too. Before reading their papers, I had thought that they were perfect students.

After months of intense mentoring from Dr. Fulford, I became fluent in middle-class language. Now, I am "bilingual". I speak the language of generational poverty (oral culture), and I speak middle-class (print culture) language. Speaking a language requires being literate about the culture and experiences that are associated with it. With an enormous amount of support from agencies and individuals (e.g. housing, food stamps, mentoring from numerous people, family support, and encouragement), I was able to move forward and become educated. Today, I can discuss topics frequently discussed by middle-class people, such as literature, politics, food and travel, or I can return to my original culture where the main topics are people, relationships and survival issues. Prior to becoming bilingual, I did not understand middle-class jokes. The references made in the jokes were unfamiliar to me. The feeling was similar to the one I had when I went to a British Comedy Club in London during my University studies. British people were laughing, and there I sat confused about what was funny.

Bob Fulford

Dr. Fulford also linked me with other professors in the University who he knew would "take care of me" and mentor me to success. One professor, Rick Seifert, a former newspaper reporter, worked with me extensively on my writing skills. Another was Dr. Barbara Gayle, a speech teacher, who encouraged me to speak about my experiences at conferences. She often spent hours working with me and found resources to pay for my trips. Cat Warren, another journalism professor, encouraged me to share my story of growing up in poverty and helped me to let go of the shame of being born into poverty. Because of Cat's mentoring, I published my first newspaper article in Portland's local newspaper, *The Oregonian*. The story went out over the Associated Press wire service and was printed all over the nation.

The doors of opportunity were continually opened for me. Because Dr. Fulford believed I was special and treated me that way, I was noticed on campus. I was selected for special activities and opportunities. He even got to know my family and helped my children get scholarships to athletic camps. When he found out that my dad loved Johnny Cash, he bought tickets for our whole family to go see his concert. When he discovered that I had never really eaten in a restaurant, he made it part of my learning to try ethnic food (now my favorite!). He visited my brother in prison and went to the parole board to help gain his release. Bob Fulford was the essential model of a mentor. He believed in me. He believed there was a way out of poverty. He met me where I was, never judging but always moving me forward. Perhaps most importantly, he linked me into a network of professionals in the community who also began exposing me to a wide range of possibilities.

Part of this mentoring meant encouraging me not to stop with a bachelor's degree. My mentors encouraged me to go for a master's degree. I said, "No way, that's for smart people." It took a long time to undo the messages that I was not smart. I began meeting people in the University setting and I would say, "What did you study?" They would reply things like, I have a master's in psychology or other discipline. I would talk with them awhile and realize that they were just people, not smarter or better–just people who had different life experiences and opportunities than I had. Once again I was empowered by the feeling that I could get a master's degree. Then, when I had attained that, my professors and mentors encouraged me to go all the way to the doctoral level.

FAMILY SUPPORT

When I told my family I was taking more classes, they would say to me, "When are you getting out?" in the same tone of voice they used with my brother who had been in prison for 12 years. My family members had never known anybody who had benefited from education. They had no frame of reference for believing that education can be a good thing or even a possibility for people like them. That did not mean they did not love me or want the best for me. They just did not have experiences that indicated that education was the best option for being successful in life.

It is a commonly held belief among educators that families living in poverty are not supportive of their children and their education. My research and my personal experiences say otherwise. Families living in poverty may have no frame of reference for education being a positive influence in their lives, but they overwhelmingly want what they see as "best" for their children. Support may mean something very different to those in poverty than it does in a middle-class society. My family supported me in many ways. They loved me. My mom and dad watched my kids while I was in school and often did my laundry and cooked for us. My dad talked with me when I was troubled and helped me parent my kids. My brothers fixed my broken-down cars or did repairs at my house. My cousins, uncles, aunts and grandma all pitched in wherever and whenever they could. There was no one prouder than they were when I received my doctorate. My entire family knows that without their contributions, I would not be Dr. Beegle. My family is living proof that it takes all kinds of support to educate students who are living in poverty.

I do not agree with the notion that people from poverty have to leave their family behind to become educated or middle-class. Harriet Goldhor Lerner (1989) writes that you cannot "not communicate with your family." She says it will impair other relationships in your lives. I did have to violate some of the values I grew up with. I was taught that if I had space on my floor, someone should be able to sleep there. If I had extra beans, someone should be eating them. If I had two dollars and you needed one, I should give it to you. When my financial aid came, I often had to lie to my family and tell them I had no money. If I gave them the financial aid granted for my educational expenses, I would not have gas to get to school or money to buy my books. Many nights I cried myself to sleep knowing that my brother's heat was shut off or my mom was out of milk and bread. I stayed sane by promising myself that some day I would be in a position to help my entire family get ahead—not just Jennifer, Daniel, and me. If I did not say no, we would all stay trapped. Even though I did have to abandon some of my values, I never abandoned my family and they never abandoned me.

Donna and brothers (1988)

JENNIFER

While I was getting my education, my daughter was also getting hers—both in school and out. As a freshman, Jennifer was offered a scholar-

Donna and brothers (2006)

ship to an elite private school, Catlin Gabel. Here, Jennifer became fluent in French and traveled to France—twice. Jennifer found a way to fit in with very privileged kids through joining the volleyball team (and later becoming captain) and through acting and directing plays. She often told me it wasn't easy fitting in with those who had so much more than we did. She would say things to the students from privilege like, "You paid what for that sweater? Do you realize that would buy someone's utilities for two months?" "Look at our science class and all this equipment. There are only seven of us in the class. In my old school, there were 45 kids, no equipment, and we shared one text book." Jennifer knew poverty first-hand. She was 14 when we finally got out of public housing and off food stamps. She had so many people she loved still living in poverty that she was compelled to help raise awareness that not everyone has the same opportunities.

At 17 and a half, Jennifer was invited to interview at Columbia University. I tried to convince her that she didn't want to go to New York. I gave her a long list of reasons why she would not like it. I did not want her to leave Oregon. She pleaded with me and showed me how she could get financial assistance to pay for the trip. Jennifer spent a week in New York. She called me after a few days and said, "Mom, I have crossed off all the reasons on your list for not liking New York. I even talked with the admissions director for two hours about poverty. I love the school. I have been writing poetry in the outside cafes, and I have been going to the theater. I LOVE NEW YORK! This is where I want to go."

One week after Jennifer came home from New York, she was killed in a car wreck. She was traveling 30 miles an hour in a 1962 Volvo on a bridge with metal grating. It was raining and, when she hit the brakes, her back tires slid causing her to spin into the other lane. She was hit by a raised truck and did not have a chance. When I lost my daughter, I also lost a huge part of me. I eternally ache for her lack of future. I ache for the changes I believe she would have made to this planet because, in so many ways, Jennifer was much wiser than I am about how we could be a more inclusive society and treat all people more humanely.

I am eternally grateful that I had her for 17 and a half years. I am especially grateful to all the people who helped our family move out of poverty—people who went beyond their job descriptions and did not judge, but truly helped us to access resources and to be exposed to possibilities. Without them, I know Jennifer would never have reached the potential she did. Most people in poverty never get to know they would love theater, or enjoy writing poetry, or have the pleasure of traveling to France. Most never get an opportunity to be all they can be. My Jennifer did. I share her story to challenge anyone working with people in poverty not to lose the "Jennifer's" in their lives.

Jennifer

MY LIFE AND FAMILY TODAY

Today, I live in Tigard, Oregon, with my husband Chuck and my two youngest children, Austin (who is eight) and Juliette (who is seven). My favorite thing in the world is talking and playing with my kids.

My son Daniel, now 23, lives minutes away. I really enjoy watching him mature and pursue his dreams. Not that long ago, he was counting silently on his fingers. I said, "Danny, what are you doing?" He said, "Mom, in 14 years, I should have my doctorate." Danny's dad has a seventh-grade education. Danny struggles with learning difficulties, but he believes in himself and is surrounded by the support needed to succeed in education.

Two of my brothers have received Bachelor's degrees. Three still struggle with literacy, but now know they can learn because their sister did. I have cousins, nieces, and nephews who are becoming educated. I have multiple cousins who grew up homeless who now have bachelor's degrees and some are entering graduate school. I have a niece who wants to be a pediatrician (not a word my family even knew before—and not someone we had ever taken our kids to!). For most of my family members, education has a new meaning. It used to mean only stress, but now it means opportunity.

Though some family members have moved out of poverty, there are still those who live on disability checks of $550 per month and minimum wage jobs. I love my family and I am very close to them. I practice what I teach in my relationships with family—I help them with everything I personally can and I build resources by connecting them to mentors and new opportunities. I am their advocate when systems that are set up to help them are not meeting their needs.

Professionally, all of my work is de-voted to ending poverty. I am President of Communication Across Barriers, a consulting firm devoted to improv-ing relationships and communication across class, race, and gender barriers. I am also the founder and program chair of PovertyBridge, a Portland based non-profit that is focused on building oppor-tunities to help people in poverty have a chance to succeed. I speak, train, and consult nationwide with anyone who works

**Donna, husband Chuck,
Juliette, and Austin**

with or is interested in making a difference for people from poverty backgrounds and those who are currently living in poverty. I combine life experience, 17 years of working on poverty issues, and my research to help people and organizations gain better knowledge about what they can do to make a difference for those they serve.

When asked why I do this work, my response is always the same: "How can I not do it? I know too much to be silent." I know what it is like to go through life feel-

Danny and Donna

ing like there is no hope and that no one cares. I grew up watching the people I loved not being treated very well by people in organizations that were supposed to help them. I saw my mom cry time after time when she was told she did not have the right paperwork or correct identifica-tion to get food or shelter. I saw my dad work 16 hours and be reduced to tears when his pay would not cover the rent and groceries for our family. I saw my grandma sleep on the ground in a cherry field, exhausted from picking since three a.m. I watched my brothers try to hide their fear

and anger when they saw our parents could not get any help to feed us—the fear and anger that eventu-ally led some of them to the justice system. I cried my heart out when the judge sentenced my beloved middle brother and best friend to prison. I hurt to my core when I saw the fear on my six-year-old child's face when we were evicted and became homeless. I will always do work that makes a difference for those who have not had genuine opportunity. I learned this not only from my experience, but from the example set by my friend and mentor, Dr. Bob Fulford.

**Donna's brothers
Rick and Wayne**

Dr. Bob Fulford died of a heart attack the day I received my Doctorate degree. At his service were so many of Bob's previous students who were like me: steeped in an oral culture, mostly from poverty, ill equipped for the traditional education system. One after another those students told stories of Bob making them feel as though they were smart, making them believe they could succeed, building the supports and networks to make it happen, and seeing only their strengths and not their weaknesses. Many people would say that it was not Bob Fulford's job to teach a junior in college not to say "ain't" and how to write a sentence. Bob often said, "I go to work every day to educate. For Donna Beegle, that meant something a little different than for other students. It meant starting where she was and keeping the high expectation that she would become educated." He would then tell anyone who would listen, "The real question is, did she get educated?" With a grin, he'd nod and say, "And then some."

I share my education and work successes, those I experienced because of the help of Bob Fulford and the many others along the way who stepped outside of their job descriptions, because everyday too much potential is lost—too many people in poverty never have a chance. Everyday, their potential is thrown away when we do not think outside of the box, nor consider the context of poverty and ask, "Am I setting people up for success?" Herbert Gans says in his book, *War on the Poor*, we keep asking people in poverty conditions to act middle class when they do not have the resources to do so. What we have to do to help people in poverty reach their potential may not be in our job description. It may not be what we are trained to do. But if we are clear about why we are in a helping profession, we are much more likely to do the right thing as opposed to doing what we have always done. If we are clear about why we go to work and what outcomes we seek to achieve, we will do what Lisbeth Schorr advocates in her book, *Within Our Reach: Breaking the Cycle of Disadvantage* (1988). That is, we will provide a comprehensive, flexible approach that meets people where they are, not where we want them to be.

Understanding Poverty

The overriding belief in the United States is that people are making a "choice" to be in poverty. The prevailing view is that education is there if you want it and you can get a good job if you work hard. Daily life experiences and how we get our information shape the ways in which we relate to one another, our expectations, and how we experience the world. The reality is that the context into which we are born and grow up shapes our view of what is possible. It selects, reflects, and defines our values, thus creating our worldview. People born into poverty are handed a different description of reality than those born with privilege and resources.

The focus of life when you live in poverty is directed towards subsistence and safety issues: basic survival necessities. Where will we sleep tonight? What will we eat? Can we find a way to keep our heat and lights turned on? Whose car got towed? Whose license got suspended for no insurance? Can I trust people outside my inner circle? The major focus is on making it through the day. People are taught to make do with what they have. Education is a luxury that makes no sense when you can't pay rent or buy food. Good jobs seem far out of reach and you have likely never met someone who has one.

People born into privilege tend to focus on self-development: What is the best education possible? What extra-curricular activities will help in reaching one's full potential? What is the best health care plan? What is the best neighborhood? They are often taught to dream and believe anything is possible. Education and good jobs are an expectation.

In 1943, Abraham Maslow proposed a psychological theory of human motivation, where he categorized human needs in a hierarchy that starts with basic needs and ends in self-actualization. The basic concept is that the higher needs in this hierarchy are more likely to come

MASLOW'S HIERARCHY OF NEEDS

Self-Actualization

Esteem

Love—Belonging

Safety

Physiological Survival

into focus once all the needs that are lower on the pyramid are mainly or entirely satisfied.

Physiological needs are all the things the body needs to maintain itself, including food, drink, air, sleep, and so on. Having safety needs met consists of feeling secure and out of danger. Belonging and love mean being accepted by and affiliated with others. Esteem needs include achievement, being competent, and gaining approval and recognition. Maslow argued that those who had basic needs met would strive for the higher order, self-actualization needs of finding self-fulfillment and realizing one's potential. Even having some of the basics of safety, acceptance and nutrition allow individuals a greater chance of learning and growing.

Individuals in poverty are often fighting for their basic physiological and safety needs. In the context of poverty, motivation and utmost aspiration, like most of us, is to reach the third level of the pyramid and feel love and acceptance by those with whom they are in relationships. This is why many young people join gangs—they want to belong. Their daily focus of making sure their survival needs are met, however, consumes energy and can take away the hope of ever meeting esteem or self-actualizing needs.

Poverty Realities: Shattering Common Myths

"Unfortunately, many Americans live on the outskirts of hope—some because of their poverty, and some because of their color, and all too many because of both. Our task is to help replace despair with opportunity. This administration today, here and now, declares unconditional war on poverty in America." —President Lyndon Johnson (State of the Union Address, 1964)

POVERTY IN NUMBERS

Although President Lyndon Johnson declared war on poverty forty years ago and at tempted to bring the nation's attention and resources to tackle the problem in the United States, poverty still persists.

Currently the United States has the highest childhood poverty rate among the 25 richest industrialized nations, with a poverty rate of 22 percent, 20 points from Denmark who had the lowest poverty rate (UNICEF, 2005). In the article, The Poverty Quagmire, the author wrote "poor children in France, Germany, and the Nordic countries are six times more likely to escape poverty than their American counterparts" (Smeeding, 2003). According to the latest census report, 37 million Americans, representing 12.7 percent of the population, live below the federal poverty guideline (U.S. Census Bureau, 2005). They reside in an "invisible nation" that has a population equal in size to that of Canada. There are some variations among states. The poorest state was Mississippi with a staggering 22 percent poverty rate.

New Hampshire and Connecticut had the lowest poverty rates at 8 percent, while Oregon was at 12.1 percent.

POVERTY RATE PER REGION		
Region	Number Below Poverty	Percentage
Nationally	37,000,000	12.7%
Northeast	6,233,000	11.6 %
Midwest	7,538,000	11.6%
South	14,798,000	14.1%
West	8,429,000	12.6%
Source: U.S. Census Bureau, current population survey, 2005 annual social and economic supplements		

What makes the above numbers even more tragic is that the indicator—the Federal poverty guideline (see table below)—used to determine the number of people in poverty is believed to underestimate the number of people in poverty (Berliner, 2005).

FEDERAL POVERTY GUIDELINE, 2005		
Family Type	Poverty Guideline	Hourly Income
1 person	$9,570	$4.60
2 persons	$12,830	$6.17
3 persons	$16,090	$7.74
4 persons	$19,350	$9.30
5 persons	$22,610	$10.87
Source: U.S. Census Bureau, current population survey		

The problem with this guideline is that it falls short of reflecting the realities of today. First, it is based on a 1960s cost of living formula. In a 1955 government study, it was reported that Americans spent approximately one-third of their after-tax income on food. A bureaucrat in the Social Security Administration took the Department of Agriculture's lowest food plan for an American family–one designed for temporary or emergency use when funds were low"—and multiplied by a factor of three to create the Federal Poverty Guideline (Hammond, 2005). Second, in the 1960s, the federal agency reports indicated that Americans spent one-third of their income on food. This figure was multiplied by a factor of three to create the Federal Poverty Guideline. It does not account for the changes in family dynamics and basic survival needs that have occurred since the 1960s. For example, more women are in the workplace now, creating a need for childcare and transportation that was not commonplace a half century ago. Both of these huge family expenses are totally ignored by the use of this formula.

The Economic Policy Institute (Ehrenreich, 2002) found (based on today's cost of living) that a person with two children would need $30,000 just to cover basic needs; including health care, transportation and daycare. Third, the current federal guidelines don't account for the rising cost of housing that has lead to a greater share of the income (33 percent) going towards providing shelter. According to a 2004 study by the Department of Housing and Urban Development, the average rent for a two-bedroom apartment nationally is $750 per month. This same study found only one place in the country where people earning minimum wage could afford a modest two-bedroom apartment; a tiny town in Georgia. Everywhere else, people in poverty are frequently getting evicted; living in motels, campers, cars, or storage sheds; or moving in with other family members.

The reality in the U.S. is that there are far too many people who struggle to meet their basic needs. The rate of hunger among people in poverty in the United States is extremely high, especially when it is compared to those of other industrialized nations (Berliner, 2005). In 2003, about 12.5 million households (around 36 million people) suffered from food insecurity. About four million of those households, or around 9.5 million people, actually went hungry some time in that year, with one-third of this group experiencing chronic hunger. Seventeen percent of the house-holds with food insecurity have children (NWAF Report).

LIVING WAGE RATES IN THE NORTHWEST, 2000		
	Living Wage for a Single Adult*	Living Wage for a Single Adult with Two Children*
Idaho	$21,037	$32,920
Montana	$20,589	$33,786
Oregon	$22,985	$37,336
Washington	$23,401	$38,500
Source: Northwest Policy Center, Northwest Job Gap Study, 2001		
*In 2000, living wage rates for a single adult ranged from $9.90 an hour in Montana to $11.25 an hour in Washington.		
**In 2000, living wage rates for a single adult with two children ranged from $15.83 in Idaho to $18.51 an hour in Washington.		

In 2004, the income deficit for families in poverty, defined as the difference between the family's income and its poverty threshold, averaged $7,775 (Census, 2005). Of those identified as living in poverty, many are living in desperate conditions and try-ing to survive on an income that is far below the official poverty threshold.

In 2004, the number of people living at half the income of the poverty threshold was 15.6 million, representing 5.4 percent of the total population and 42.3 per-cent of the tens of millions of people who are officially classified as "the poor" (U.S. Bureau of the Census, 2005). These are the poorest of those in poverty, and one third of these are children. People who fall in this bracket of income are re-ferred to as "hard to serve" by social workers and "under class" by Myrdal (1962) and Auletta (1993). They are the least likely to break the poverty barriers and live stable financial lives, struggling to come out of an entrenched generational situation (Beegle, 2000). There are no official statistics or commonly agreed upon criteria to determine the number of people who are trapped in generational poverty. This contributes to keeping their plight from being recognized and reduces their chances of escaping poverty.

Examination of the census bureau poverty rate trend since the 1990s shows that over the decade of the 1990s the rate of poverty was reduced to almost 2.5 percent nationally. Unfortunately, the expansion of jobs and the income growth of that period stopped at the end of the 1990s. Most of the gain that had been made to reduce the poverty rate has been lost. With the sharp increase in housing prices, no noticeable increases in real wages for people in poverty, an economic expansion that has failed to create living-wage jobs, and a reduction in tax revenues that resulted in a reduction of aid to people in poverty, the poverty rate continues to climb (Berliner, 2005).

SHATTERING COMMON MYTHS ABOUT POVERTY

In his 1961 inaugural address, President John F. Kennedy said:

> *"The great enemy of the truth is very often not the lie–deliberate, contrived, and dishonest, but the myth–persistent, persuasive, and unrealistic."*
> *(www.jfklibrary.org)*

There is a prevalent lack of understanding about poverty and about people who suffer under its cruel conditions. Building a foundation for understanding poverty requires us to address the common myths often attached to this issue.

Myth: Poverty is solely a minority issue. Poverty is often perceived as a race or ethnic issue. It is commonly described as a problem that is associated with racism. Actually, some minorities are indeed over-represented among those in poverty, but not all. Compared to an overall poverty rate of 12.7 percent, for example, about 25 percent of Blacks were categorized as "poor" in 2004 and about 22 percent in that same category were Hispanic. For Asians, however, the figure was 8 percent. This compares to a poverty rate of 8.6 percent for Whites. In total numbers, though, it is important to note that the majority (close to 47 percent) of people in poverty in the United States are White, with a total number of almost 17 million in 2004 (US Census, 2005).

NUMBER IN POVERTY AND POVERTY RATES BY RACE/ETHNICITY, 2004		
Race/Ethnicity	Number	Poverty Rate
All races	35,997,000	12.7%
White alone or in combination	25,301,000	10.8%
White alone, not Hispanic	16,870,000	8.6%
Black alone	9,000,000	24.7%
Asian alone	1,209,000	9.8%
Hispanic (of any race)	9,132,000	21.9%
Source: U.S. Census Bureau, Current Population Survey, 2005		

Research studies on poverty often ignore the White people in poverty. Educational and public service professionals and organizations frame their services in a manner that does not account for the unique needs and situations of White people in poverty. Poverty needs to be acknowledged as a large-scale societal problem that cuts across racial/ethnic lines, and special attention should be paid to the voices and needs of those in poverty who have often been marginalized, ignored, and treated as invisible.

Myth: Government assistance is adequate to the extent that it encourages independence. Contrary to this myth, people in poverty in the United States are not and cannot get out of poverty by relying on Government assistance. In his 2003 article *The Poverty Quagmire,* Timothy Smeeding wrote:

> "We in America have high child poverty rates because we choose to, not because we cannot do anything about it. Other nations make different choices and get different results. For example, Tony Blair lifted Britain's spending on poor families with children by 0.9 percent of GDP. The result? Britain's high child poverty rate is ebbing as ours continue to climb. The United States could commit half the effort of Tony Blair's government and see a seismic shift in the well-being of millions of children. The truth is that America tolerates—even accepts—persistent child poverty" (Smeeding, 2003).

Nationally, the average welfare check for one parent and two children in 2005 was $478 per month. Twenty years ago, it was $408. The two percent annual cost of living raise added to the disability check is taken off of the food stamps allotment of about 83¢ per person per meal. The 2 percent annual cost of living raise added to the disability check is taken off of the food stamps allotment, already a meager amount of money given the basic expenses for housing, food, and health care needs. Despite a commonly held, but misinformed, belief that people in poverty have babies to get more welfare, the monthly welfare check only increases, on average, about $60 if you have a baby. In some states, such as Idaho, no additional money is added to the welfare check after the second child is born. In other states, the support increases only slightly. For instance, in North Carolina the amount increases $25 to support the new baby.

In 1986, I applied for welfare and was given $408 per month plus minimal food stamps for my two children and me. With rent at $395, I had just $13 dollars left each month for transportation, clothing, utilities, the Laundromat, soap, shampoo, and other basic necessities. When I decided to pay the utilities rather than the full rent, my welfare worker said that I needed money management classes so I could stop being evicted!! The message to me was strong: I was doing something wrong. This is the same message I got from working. I worked hard all my life. I did migrant labor work, worked in fast food, and worked in factories. None of the minimum wage jobs available to someone like me, with limited skills, provided me with a living wage for my little family.

The available assistance from government and social services barely helps people in poverty cope with their poverty conditions, let alone break loose from its grip. Researchers conducting a recent study by a consortium of Illinois universities, in partnership with the Metro Chicago Information Center (Lewis et. al., 2005), interviewed a representative sample of more than 1,000 women who were former welfare recipients. The study findings indicated that approximately 50 percent of those initially interviewed for the study were working, and that the proportion receiving TANF (temporary assistance for needy families) cash benefits dropped from 53 percent to 11 percent over four years. However, five years into welfare reform in Illinois, these former welfare recipients may still be working, but they were frequently still living in poverty (Lewis et. al, 2005). According to various state Leaver studies, former welfare recipients earn an average $8,000 to $12,000 annually (Jarchow, 2002).

Instead of providing support, the current welfare policies create additional barriers, even to those struggling to get out of poverty. When I was presented with the opportunity to go to school, I was notified that the state welfare policies dictate that in order to qualify for welfare I needed to be available for any minimum wage job. If I were in school, I would not be available. If I went to school, the government would sanction me and cut my welfare check from $408 to $258. This policy is still in effect in all but five states today. As I sat there crying in the welfare office, I began calculating how my kids and I could survive on $258 a month. I did not know what was ahead, but I knew I did not want to stay in the world of welfare and poverty. I told the welfare worker to "go ahead and cut my check" if that's what she had to do. I was going to school! I could only say that because I was one of the lucky few who received help with housing costs. Only 14% of those who qualify for housing assistance receive it. Others are put on a wait list or turned away.

The battle to move out of poverty is not only a challenge for those coming from generational poverty, but also for those on the margins. If a person happens to fall into poverty because of a divorce, illness, or job loss (the three most common reasons for falling into situational poverty), their chances of getting back out of poverty in the U.S. are considerably less than in many other countries. Berliner (2005) points out that while the rate of people who fall into poverty in the United States is comparable to that of some of the richest nations, the U.S. has the highest percentage of those who become permanently trapped in poverty, suggesting that the United States has fewer effective mechanisms in place to pull these people out of poverty once they have fallen in it. We are a leader among the rich nations of the world in terms of failing to help people exit poverty (Berliner, 2005). Not only does the current system of support fail to help people in generational poverty exit from poverty, it does not bode well for those who might experience a turn of luck in their living conditions, either.

Typically, despite the fact that government assistance falls short of covering people's basic needs, many people often cling to it because they see no options for earning money for survival with their skills and education levels. They often have so internalized their poverty as a personal deficiency that they see no hope for anything but welfare or disability (Beegle, 2000).

Myth: Social mobility is possible. All people have to do to pull themselves out of poverty is work hard. There is a dominant belief in our society that if individuals work hard enough they will do well. Social mobility is portrayed as a real possibility for all those with a high work ethic. Unfortunately two-thirds of people living in poverty are working an average of 1.7 jobs (U.S. Census, 2004). One in four workers earn poverty level wages, i.e., less than $8.84 an hour (Business Week, 2004). There are a lot of people working hard and still not making it. Nationally, one in four working families is struggling, and 27 percent have incomes below 200 percent of the poverty level (Casey Foundation, 2003). In Oregon, more than one fourth (27 percent) of families in poverty work full-time, year round and are still in poverty (OCPP, 2004). The author of the article, *The Poverty Quagmire,* wrote, "fully one-third of children of single mothers in the United States today are not just poor but extremely poor. As the study data indicate, low-income single mothers in the United States work more hours than do single mothers in any other wealthy nation, yet have higher poverty rates" (Smeeding, 2003).

Statistics on job advancement clearly show that for many people there is little, if any, correlation between hard work and wage increase (Beegle, 2000). If an individual has a high school diploma or less and takes a minimum wage job, the research shows that in 10 years, on average, the income will increase just $2.00 per hour. Then after working another 15 years, the hourly rate will increase only $.25 more—totaling an increase of $2.25 in 25 years. For example:

> Oregon's minimum wage (2006): $7.50
> Work 10 years: $9.50
> Work 25 years: $9.75

The United for a Fair Economy and the Institute for Policy Studies have calculated that if the minimum wage had risen at the same rate of CEO pay since 1990, it would stand at $23 an hour—but, instead, it has only risen from $3.80 to $5.15. Thus proving, it does not matter how hard you work! Hard work alone does not increase income. The American labor market rewards people who are educated or skilled. Who works harder, the migrant labor worker, or the person in their cubicle? If you work hard cleaning hotel rooms and you finish all your rooms, what else do you get? Another room to clean.

After the first 10 years of working in primarily physical-labor jobs, using their bodies to earn a living instead of using their minds, physical health begins to give out, making workers less employable. They become a corporate risk. No one wants to hire them. Employers would rather have someone younger, stronger, healthier, and less likely to have an illness or injury on the job. People who use their bodies to earn a living are out of the labor market 15 years ahead of those who use their minds. If people are struggling to pay rent, buy food and working, the chances that they can go to school or get more training are slim. Programs to support increasing education or skills for those in poverty are few and, if they do exist, they are generally not set up to help people meet the needs of housing, utilities, etc. while they are in training or school. That gap results in the lucky few who get training or education support "dropping out" to deal with the crisis of poverty.

Myth: Education—the only sure way to help people out of poverty—is readily available and accessible to all people. Most people believe education is there if you want it. But, according to the National Institute of Early Education Research, less than 60 percent of eligible children were served by Head Start programs—the programs which are usually children's first opportunity for a quality education (Barnett, et. al. 2004). A report from the National Center for Children in Poverty declared that Head Start can promote the pursuit of higher education among the next generation of parents. They found that low-income children who attend Head Start are more likely to graduate from high school and attend college. They further wrote, "Protecting the funding and high standards of Head Start will ensure that more low-income children are able to pursue higher education—and the economic security that comes with it" (Koball and Douglas-Hall, 2004).

Furthermore, if you come from poverty, you have very likely never identified with people who benefited from education. Education may be seen as a place where you don't belong or a place where you are punished for your poverty. It is difficult to value something when you don't have a frame of reference that it is for people like you.

A college education appears to be the only possibility to help people break the walls of poverty and escape its hardships. There is a considerable jump in the earning power that comes with obtaining a college education. A person with a high school diploma in the United States earns on average $17,000 a year. Even one year of college can increase one's income. Piercy, et. al. (1998) found the two-year college degree increased income of participants by 65 percent over that of high school graduates. A person with a bachelor's degree earns on average $40,000 a year (national average). Research literature shows that most people with bachelor's degrees may start out at a low wage, but will earn a living wage (as defined by the median income for a family of four) over the course of their career (Jones, 1998; Mortenson, 1995, 1998). However, only 26 percent of the population holds a bachelor's degree (Mortenson, 1998).

Although we all know that education matters in the country's economy, people living in poverty are the least likely to become educated (Mortenson, 1996). People in poverty face substantial barriers both in schools and colleges (Beegle, 2000). Recently, Anyon (2005) also pointed out:

> Currently, relatively few urban students from poverty backgrounds go past ninth grade. The graduation rates in large comprehensive inner-city high schools are abysmally low. In 14 such New York City schools, for example, only 10 to 20 percent of ninth graders in 1996 graduated four years later. Despite the fact that low-income individuals desperately need a college degree to find decent employment, only seven percent obtain a bachelor's degree by age twenty-six. So, in relation to the needs of low-income students, urban districts fail their students with more egregious consequences now than in the early twentieth century (page 69).

Similarly, access to higher education is becoming increasingly harder given the rising cost of college education and the reduction in available scholarships. Mortenson's [1993] research on access to college shows that it is less likely today for a person born into poverty to get an education than it was in the 1940s. Although some progress has been made in diminishing the educational barriers of race, gender, geography, and religion, poverty is the one barrier that has not been overcome. In 1970, a person from the lowest income quartile was only 16 percent as likely to complete a bachelor's degree as a person from the highest income quartile. By 1989, that rate had fallen to 11 percent (Mortensen, 1991), and was at 10 percent in 1996 (Levine & Nidiffer, 1996, Mortenson, 1996). Since then, an even lower percentage of the poorest people in the U.S. have become educated (Valadez, 1998; Greenberg, Strawn, & Plimpton, 1999).

For nearly half a century, the association of social and economic disadvantage to the persisting achievement gap has been well known to economists, sociologists and educators. Most, however, have avoided the obvious implication of this understanding: raising the achievement of lower-class children requires the amelioration of the social and economic conditions of their lives, not just educational and school reform (Rothstein, p. 11, cited in Berliner, 2005). Rubin (1970) said it well, school contact is not long enough or strong enough to break the injures inflicted by living in poverty conditions. While educators can and should better meet the needs of students in poverty, they need the help and support from the entire community. No child left behind will require housing, food, health care, safe places to play and a caring community to support the child and the family.

Our goal as a society should go beyond focusing narrowly on schools and the opportunities for social mobility that they might open. Our commitment should be to work together until we reach the point where every person living in the United States—this fortunate land of abundance—can live with dignity, have basic needs met, and have his or her human potential nurtured towards the limitless capacity all humans carry within themselves. As a country, we need to have responsive schools, as well as have measures in place to "rescue" those that fall into poverty, and make sure they never get trapped in its devastating condition. It is a shame that in a country with so many resources we allow so much potential to be lost. The next page offers you an opportunity to explore the realities people in poverty face.

ACTIVITY 1: PAYING BILLS

You are the sole support of your family that includes your 5-year-old child and an infant. You work 40 hours per week, making $8.50 an hour. Because you have no high school education and limited skills, this is the best job you have had in years. Please look at the list of bills and expenses for this month (which total $3,267) and decide how you will spend your income. In the Paid/Not column indicate which bills you will pay by writing in the amount you will pay. In the comment section, write any additional comments on other ways you may handle this (cancel service, sell items to come up with money, pay half this month/half next, etc.). (Note: Because you make too much money, you are not qualified for any federal or state assistance.)

	Amount	Paid/Not	Comment
Monthly Income (after taxes)	**$1,307**	--	
Apartment Rent	$700		
Birthday Party Gift: Your child is invited to a friend's party	$10		
Cable Television	$25		
Car Insurance: Final notice	$150		
Daycare: For two kids.	$400		
Diapers: Out of diapers.	$15		
Electric Bill: Final notice before shut off.	$250		
Field Trip: Activity fee and sack lunch Teacher also needs chaperones.	$10		
Gasoline	$100		
Groceries	$400		
Garbage Service	$39		
Health Insurance: You work for a small company, you have an option of buying your own family health insurance.	$900		
Laundromat	$30		
Phone Bill	$49		
Rent to Own Payment	$25		
Shampoo and Soap: Out of both.	$6		
Shoes: Child has outgrown their shoes.	$20		
Snacks for School: Your child's week to supply store-bought snacks for class.	$40		
Toilet Paper: Out of toilet paper.	$8		
Water Bill: Final notice before shut off.	$90		

Reflection on Bill Paying Activity

Recognizing that this is a simulated activity and can not fully compare the experience of not having enough, please respond to the following questions:

- How did it feel to have so few resources to take care of your family's needs?

- How did you prioritize what you were going to pay and what you were going to ignore?

- If the bill was something your child needs/wants, how would you explain your decisions to them?

- How could you manage your money to make things work better for you?

- How could you make life better for yourself and your family?

Defining Social Class Experiences

One will not fully be able to understand and appreciate the circumstances and situations that affect those in poverty without first having a good understanding of basic social class structures. Social class refers to relative social rank in terms of income, wealth, status, life chances, and/or power.

Perhaps the most profound and lasting understanding of the complexities of class status came from the writings of Max Weber (1946). Social class in a Weberian sense may be seen as comprising three distinct although related dimensions regarding the impact of social class on lifestyle, context, and economic opportunity. The Weberian social-class framework examines family social status (education, occupation, connections, and income) as well as individual ability and critical intervening experiences. His philosophical and theoretical perspectives of social-class theory shifts the "blame" of poverty from the individual and emphasizes inequalities, power and advantage.

To some extent, Weber (1946) agreed with Karl Marx that class could be defined in economic or market terms. He added that class could also be determined by how much a person had and how much she or he was likely to get (his or her life chances). Weber drew attention to the different kinds of property owned, the way property was distributed, and a person's status and power relations. He argued that although property and lack of property are the two basic categories of all class situations, further distinctions existed.

Weber (1946) explained that status groups (classes) are phenomena that result from the distribution of power within a community. He believed a person's power or lack thereof would affect his or her social status. Status included everything associated with what Weber called "societal honor" that required people to live a specific lifestyle, including language, social conventions, rituals, patterns of economic consumption, understandings regarding and relations with outsiders, and matters of taste in food, clothing, grooming, and hair style. Each status group is set apart by where (and how) they live—each listens to different music, eats different foods, reads different materials, relates to others differently, thinks differently, has different expectations, has different relationships to power, faces different experiences, and so on.

The respective status or class norms can be worlds apart. In addition, if an individual is not living in the style expected, he or she is looked upon as deficient, or pushed away as an outsider. Membership into a social class is determined by an individual's ability to identify with and respond to a complex set of expectations shaped by the values, beliefs and habits of its members. Often, individuals from a certain social class interact exclusively with each other. As a result, the expectations of people living in poverty reflect the expectations of those with whom they identify and interact the most: others in poverty, which is indeed a factor in limiting their prospects of breaking through the boundaries of their social class.

Weber (1946) also emphasized the importance of focusing on social class to explore life chances, opportunities for income, and intergenerational social mobility. Weber believed that it was necessary to examine the social structure in which people live to fully understand a person's life chances. Weber suggested that the way property was distributed shaped life chances; thus, people with little or no property receive little or no opportunity, while people with more property receive more opportunities. He believed that in a capitalist society, if a person were born into a lower class, his or her class status would serve as an **IRON CAGE,** preventing him or her from gaining access to most of the opportunities for upward mobility. Weber also noted that people in certain classes were privileged through education and those with no education experienced difficulty in competing in the labor market.

Weber's social class theory is illustrated by a 2004 study, The National Center for Children in Poverty reviewed the data surrounding the effects of parental education on income. From their findings, they surmised that higher education is one of the most effective ways that parents can raise their families' incomes. They found clear evidence that more highly educated parents have higher earnings. In addition, if parents have low education levels, full-time employment does not protect their families from low incomes. Among children whose parents work full-time and year-round:

- 73 percent of children whose parents do not have a high school degree live in low-income families

- 43 percent of children whose parents have a high school degree, but no college education, live in low-income families

- Only 15 percent of children whose parents have at least some college education live in low-income families

As Weber noted, education matters and people from the lower classes are the least likely to obtain it.

Although Weber's theory addressed some of the complexities of poverty, no one theoretical framework can completely describe the life experiences of those living in poverty (Bane & Ellwood, 1994). The fact that people experiencing underclass poverty present a wide array of personalities, backgrounds, experiences, and life chances (Levine & Nidiffer, 1996; London, 1992) makes any attempt at defining social class and types of poverty challenging and controversial. However, defining the characteristics of a particular social class helps us make sense of the daily realities, lived conditions, and worldviews of its members; thus providing an insight into why people occupy their position in a certain class. Not paying attention to social class and its implications erases the struggles of people in poverty from our collective consciousness. It diverts attention from the structural and political causes of these struggles, and keeps us trapped in a vicious circle of blaming and focusing on deficiencies. Focusing on the commonalities that emerge illuminates the realities of people living in poverty and improves our chances to understand their needs and successfully respond to them.

From Poverty to Wealth:
The Wide Variety of Social Classes in the United States

When social class is discussed, many people believe there are three socio-economic classes: people in poverty, the middle class, and the wealthy. But many scholars who have studied the social class structures of the United States assert that there are multiple classes and subclasses (Brantlinger, 2003; Gilbert, 2003, Grusky, 2001). For the purpose of this book, social class is presented in different categories that fall into a continuum, taking into account Weber's work and based upon the following criteria: amount of income, amount and type of property owned, extent of housing and job stability, type of resources available, social status, and life chances. The length of time one spends in poverty is also used to further categorize poverty into long term and temporary/situational poverty.

Poverty can be long term or temporary, specific to certain situations that people find themselves in for a specific period of time. When discussing long-term poverty, there are two groups of people who are situated in this class: those in generational poverty and the working poor. Wilson (1996) offered a useful distinction between the working poor and underclass (generational) poverty. According to Wilson, people experiencing long-term poverty often share the experiences of underemployment, unemployment, labor-force dropouts, weak marriages, and single parenthood (Wilson, 1996). However, those in underclass poverty are more likely to survive on day labor, temporary seasonal migrant work, and funds received from unemployment, disability, welfare, social security, and underground activities (Wilson, 1987). These methods of survival create experiences that make it hard for people to focus on anything but basic needs.

What further differentiates working poor from generational poverty is that adults in the "working poor" category work more often and are generally not eligible for federal assistance. The experiences of the working poor differs from those in generational poverty in that there is most often some income in the families of the working poor, albeit in low-status, low-paying minimum-wage jobs that rarely pay enough to meet needs and rarely offer opportunities for moving up. Since our society values work, there is some status that comes with working. If someone says, "I work 40 hours a week at Walmart," the general response is "At least you have a job." There is also a small sense of control. If you work 40 hours at McDonalds, they have to pay you or there is legal recourse. Those who survive on disability or welfare can have their checks taken away or held up because they do not having the correct ID or paperwork. The caseworker has the power. This reinforces a perspective that "life happens to you." Wilson (1996) suggested that because people who are working know there is a check coming, even though they struggle, they are accustomed to having more control over some of their destiny than those in generational poverty. Families in generational poverty may also be working in the "underground" economy. They get paid "under the table" or with no paper train or taxes. If the employer, in this instance, "decides" not to pay you, you have no recourse.

GENERATIONAL POVERTY

The harsh conditions of generational poverty may keep these families from breaking the barriers for generations.

- These families have incomes insufficient to meet their basic human needs and are in jobs that are highly unstable such as seasonal, migrant, or day labor. They often rely on Federal Aid when not employed.

- These families have never owned land, nor have they ever owned anything that has real value. Their "ownership," if any, has always been of depreciable assets, that is, things that become less valuable over time.

Four generations of Donna's family

- No one in the immediate circle of these families has benefited from education, nor has been promoted or was respected in a job. Because of this, they lack of a "safety net"—a circle of family, friends, or associates with the access to knowledge and resources for moving out of poverty.

- These families are highly mobile, often migrating to where jobs are or being evicted due to lack of adequate resources.

- Being in school and facing its demands is in sharp contradiction with the pressures and realities of their lives. This split in focus results in a strong disconnect with their schooling experience, often leading to a high level of drop-out and school problems.

- For these families, the primary focus is on survival and making it through the day.

- People living in generational poverty often fear police and may be angry at authority figures who hold power over them and their loved ones.

- Their poverty is seen by many as a personal deficiency. They receive strong messages from society that they are to blame for their poverty conditions. People in generational poverty "internalize" the blame and, like others in America, are rarely aware of the structural and systemic causes of poverty.

"WORKING" POOR

- These families live paycheck to paycheck, often in fear of being laid off or having hours cut.

- Their focus is often on making it two weeks or a month at a time.

- After housing expenses are met, there is little money for other needs or for any extras.

- Most do not own property.

- Very few have health insurance/regular health care and, due to the inaccurate federal poverty guideline, they are ineligible for any assistance.

- High school graduation is often seen as an unattainable goal.

- Poverty is seen as a personal deficiency. They have bought into the American belief that if they work hard, they will move up and succeed. This has not happened because they lack education and/or training to earn a living wage. Assumptions are made that they must not have been smart enough or worked hard enough and those are the reasons that they are barely getting by.

- Children are often confused that parents are working but the can not have or do what their peers have and do. This confusion often results in anger at the parent for "not doing enough."

WORKING CLASS

- These families generally work with their hands. They may use their minds for work, but generally not as policy-makers and decision-makers.

- Their incomes depend on hourly wages for their labor.

- Adults have stable employment. Status and pay in their work varies from low to high within their own work community. Some working class people are very skilled and make great wages and are very well respected/have high status in their field.

- Some own property.

- Most hope that at least one child will attend college.

TEMPORARY/SITUATIONAL POVERTY

- People who experience temporary or situational poverty usually have grown up in a stable environment surrounded by people who are educated and able to earn a living wage, have had a solid safety net, have attended school regularly, and have had health care. They then have a crisis (health, divorce, etc.) that results in an income drop. They generally are able to make it back to middle class.

- They have not internalized the poverty as their own fault, but blame poverty on the situation.

Two specific examples of situational poverty in the United States:

Depression Era Poverty (1929-1939)
- A time when the societal message was, "We are all in this together," even though social class differences existed during the depression.

- Poverty was seen as societal problem and was not internalized as a personal deficiency.

- There were still social class differences such as some people had more land than others and some people had more sugar than others.

Immigrant Poverty

- These families often come to the United States because they were taught that the U.S. is the "land of opportunity."

- Some possess few or no resources, and most experience language and culture barriers.

- They seem to do better than people born into poverty in the United States, because they view poverty as a systemic problem and not their personal problem (Freire, 1970).

Note: If they do not make it out of poverty in a generation, they too begin to internalize the poverty and attribute their failure to get out of poverty to their personal failings.

These families generally have a degree of economic independence, but not a great deal of social power in their society. The breadwinners usually have a higher education and/or specialized skills that bring higher income and more security and stability than those of working class people. There are many categories under middle class:

- Lower (Aspiring) Middle-Class: Portion with lower and less stable income due to less education and/or skills, or unstable employment. Adults imitate neighbors with consumer purchases. They fear the loss of their property values. Going to college is emphasized with children.

- Solidly Middle-Class: Own home and have investments or business. Assume children will be college graduate/professionals. Adults may have season tickets to some sporting or entertainment events.

- Upper-Middle-Class: Portion with higher income due to professional jobs and/or investment incomes. Families usually send their children to private schools to prepare them for college. They may have a security system in house and belong to a "club." They are likely to view local police as protectors of property. They hire others to care for their kids. They may have collections of rare and expensive art or artifacts.

"Risen from Poverty" Middle Class: Solidly middle-income right now, but still lack the "safety net". If they fell on hard times, they are not sure who (if anyone) would come to their rescue. In addition, they are the "safety net" for others (their immediate family, friends, etc.).

Illusory Middle Class: These Americans have houses, cars, TVs, etc., but they also have staggering debt associated with each thing. They are technically bankrupt. When their job runs out or the bills accumulate, they slowly slip under the financial waters and are never heard from again. Their lives shrink. Not quite poverty, but also not middle-class, either.

Millionaire Middle Class: People who have a net worth of over a million dollars, but who have not mentally accepted their wealth. May have guilt feelings, negative associations, or may just not see it.

—Sharif Abdullah, the Common Way Institute

OWNING CLASS RICH

These families own income-producing assets sufficient to make paid employment unnecessary. They are featured as "model citizens" in local newspapers and dabble in activities in the public eye. They may travel widely at any time of year. They may own at least two other homes, give parties for "celebrities" or politicians, and support charities.

RULING CLASS RICH

These people hold positions of power in major institutions of society and may live secluded lives or are protected from the general public. They travel on family-owned aircraft/boats. Adults involved in child-rearing are hired by other people hired to serve the family. Children are raised with the expectation that they too will be rich and should find something to do with their time.

UNDERSTANDING YOUR OWN SOCIAL STATUS AND EXPERIENCES WITH POVERTY

Your personal experiences and perspective on social class shape your ability to understand and see others. It is important to have a real understanding of your own social-class background and current reality if you want to be in a position to help people in poverty.

The following two activities will help you gain a better understanding of your background and life experience in terms of social class.

ACTIVITY 2: PERSONAL SOCIAL CLASS TIMELINE

On the next page is an opportunity to explore your personal "class" time line and reflect on how these experiences shaped your life as well as your interactions, attitudes and beliefs about people in poverty. As outlined in the previous pages, there are various social classes in the United States. Whichever class a person grows up in shapes his or her view of himself/herself and his or her future options.

Often, people from helping professions have grown up in some form of poverty and want to pass their wisdom onto those they work with. It is essential to understand what type of poverty you were brought up in and how it shaped your perspective of yourself and your life chances. Even if you did not grow up in poverty, it is good to look at your own social class background and think about how these experiences color the way you see people and the ways you choose to serve, communicate, and interact with them.

Instructions:

- Put in the year above the important events already outlined on the chart (the year you were born, the year you entered elementary school, the year you graduated from high school or got your GED).

- On the remaining hash marks, put in additional events (i.e. college/career, marriage, kids) that are important to your life history.

- Under the events of your life, describe the Socio-Economic Status (SES) of your family and how you know this (for example, describe what your family did for a living, the role of education in your life, whether your family owned land or were workers of the land).

- In the oval before your birth, briefly describe the SES history of your family.

- Write the names of the people who made a difference in your life near the time(s) you were in a relationship with them.

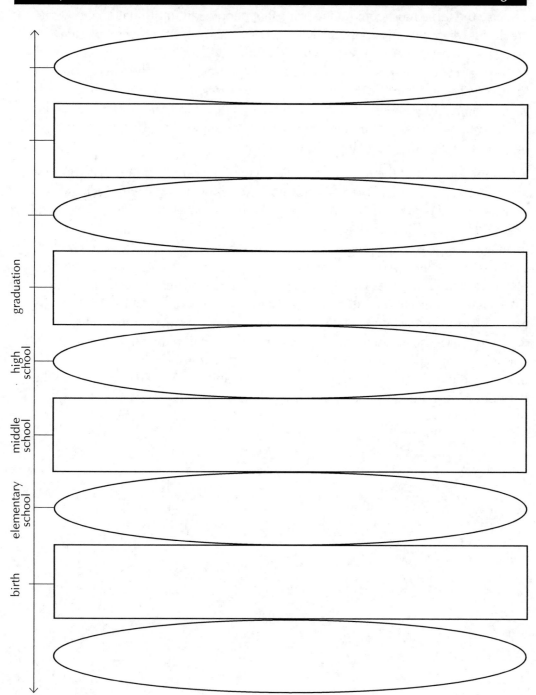

ACTIVITY 3: HOW FAR FROM POVERTY?

Because the three most common reasons that people fall into situational poverty are illness, divorce, or job loss, Activity 3, How Far From Poverty, was designed to let you see how vulnerable you might be to poverty conditions. The first part of the activity asks you to think about your current expenses and the resources you have to provide for your family. The second part of the activity asks you to imagine what would happen to your family if you were to be hit by two major losses at one time. It asks you to think about the ways you would continue to care for your family and figure out where you would turn for assistance.

When thinking about the resources available to you, you might find that you are able to turn to family and friends for assistance. People from poverty, generally, only know others in poverty. When they fall on hard times, their friends and family may also be struggling. They are forced to turn to systems and institutions to assist them and give them a helping hand. And since the systems are often themselves stretched to the limits, the assistance given keeps people from becoming completely destitute, but does not allow them to pull themselves out of their situation. Take a few minutes to fill out the following form. Use your best guesses about your actual income and expenses. If you don't have a certain expense that is listed on the chart, leave the amount and date column blank. Fill in the blank bill lines with any additional expenses you have that are not already listed. Once you have this monetary picture of your life, turn the page over and answer the questions on the back of the form. (Please note: this will not be shared with others; this is for your reflection only.)

DESCRIBE YOUR FAMILY:

	Name	Age	Monthly Income
Primary income earner			
Spouse/partner			
Children/other dependents			

MONTHLY BILLS:

	Amount	Date Due
Necessary Bills:		
Rent/Mortgage		
Electricity		
Natural Gas		
Water/Sewer		
Garbage		
Cable/Internet		
Phone		
Gas		
Food		
Car Insurance		
Life Insurance		
Miscellaneous Bills:		
Medical Bills		
Car Payment(s)		
Student Loan(s)		
Credit Cards		
Clothing (all family)		
Total		

NET WORTH:

Property	What Worth	What Owed
Home		
Car/Auto		
Other (Boats, RV, etc.)		
Retirement Account		
Savings		
Inheritance		

In case of emergency, we have enough money saved to cover all bills for at least six months: ❑ Yes ❑ No

If a natural disaster were to hit your town around the time you lose your job, how many months' worth of savings do you have set aside to support your family through the lack of work and additional expenses?

Who are the people you could call for help if you lost your job or had a personal financial crisis?

What resources can you access from family and friends to help you through (money to pay bills, a place to stay, etc.)?

If you were evicted from your home, how many places could you go? Where and with whom could you stay?

If you had no job and no money for food and no one to call, what would you do for food today?

If you had no money to buy clothing for your children to attend school or no clothes that you could wear to look for work, where would you go to get appropriate clothing?

If you could not find work and had no one to help, what would you be willing to do to help your family survive (i.e. sell the house/cars; sell other possessions—jewelry, family heirlooms, TV; ask family members to do jobs you normally would not want them to take; ask family members to give up things—sports, extracurricular activities, school—in order to get a job and help make ends meet)?

The emotions you feel as you answer these questions provide a wonderful opportunity to reflect on how you came to your ideas about people in poverty. What emotions and thoughts emerge (Fear? Anger?)? How can you use these emotions to impact your views of those who live in poverty and your ability to serve them?

Stay tuned into your beliefs, experiences, and feelings about people who live in poverty. Remember, if we judge, we cannot help. Believe and trust that people are making the best decisions possible based on their experiences, worldview and perspectives.

The Worldview Taught by Poverty

What does the world look and feel like when you are hungry, homeless, and have nowhere to turn? The experience of living in poverty shapes the values, habits, and behavior of those who have to endure its hardships and leaves them with a different perspective than those born with privilege. For a long time, researchers and professionals alike neglected to listen to the voices of people in poverty. Assumptions were made about the character and values of people living in desperate situations (Lewis, 1975). Few examined the experiences of poverty to become aware of the impact of these experiences on the way people living in poverty assign meanings to events, things, and people around them.

In 2000, as part of my doctoral dissertation work (Beegle, 2000), I conducted extended interviews with a number of college graduates who managed to break the barriers of generational poverty. Listening to these voices from generational poverty gave me a powerful insight into their daily lives and struggles for survival. It also validated my own life experience and has enriched my understanding of the worldview that emerges out of living in poverty.

Schein (1992) explains that people's beliefs and ways of doings emerge in response to the context and conditions to which they are exposed. Our human behavior is, most of the time, a reflection of the "solutions" we discovered as we responded to our environment. Our responses become what is "normal" and we often get stuck "doing what we have always done." Schein (1992) adds that the longer these solutions "work" for us the more ingrained and habitual our behavior, values, and beliefs become. Burke (1969) describes this as "trained incapacity"—basically you keep doing what you know, even if it does not work. People from all social classes experience trained incapacity. A great example of trained incapacity is the practice of homework. I have asked teachers for over a decade if homework is an effective teaching and learning strategy for students who live in poverty. After posing the question to thousands of educators, I have yet to see one hand raise and say, "Yes, it works." Overwhelmingly educators say it serves to alienate students in poverty even more. Yet, nationwide, we keep giving homework to our students in poverty.

The remaining part of this section is based on my own experience in generational poverty and on what I learned from my research (Beegle, 2000). It offers a glimpse into the world of people struggling with poverty as they see it, and into the meanings they come to associate with people and things around them. The information presented is based totally on research that I have collected from talking to and living with people who have experienced generational poverty. It is an attempt to give a voice to those who are so often unheard.

My conversations with people from generational poverty repeatedly revealed that people in poverty:

- Have internalized a great deal of shame and humiliation.

- Believe that poverty was and is seen by the rest of society as their fault.

- Feel that their lives are out of their control.

The shame of living in poverty: The impact of the poverty spills over into every aspect of the experience of living, learning, and interacting with the rest of society. Feelings of shame follow people from poverty into educational situations and into their relationships with others. The context of poverty shapes how a person feels about their appearance, where they live, what food they can afford, and the work their parents do (Beegle, 2000). These issues gain additional importance and become strong status symbols that determine whether or not they feel they are worthy enough to belong. Freire (1970) states that every society teaches its people what it takes to belong. In the United States, the neighborhood you live in, the clothing you wear, and the shoes you have matter tremendously and tell you (and others) where you belong.

APPEARANCE. People in poverty describe a world where they feel their value as human beings is judged by their appearance. Stories about appearance relate to cleanliness of themselves and family members, haircuts or styles, clothing, and shoes. These stories reflect the deep impact of the shaming messages they receive from others around them on their self-worth and sense of belonging.

"I hated school, No one liked me. Everyone could tell I was poor by my ragged clothes, horrible shoes, and free lunch tickets."—Julie

"No one wanted us around. We didn't smell good, our hair was dirty and stringy, and most people made us feel like we didn't belong."—Peggy

"I went to school one day and another kid in my class said I was wearing her shirt that her Mom had donated. I wanted to die. I hated school."—Carolyn

Comments about disliking or hating a certain place or context are often connected to an experience in which a student is humiliated or embarrassed by her or his poverty. It is not only their own personal appearances they feel embarrassed by, but also the appearances of their parents or family members. Most describe experiences where they perceive they are judged and made fun of for their parents' appearance:

"My Mom took me to a birthday party and when we got there she walked me to the door. The other Moms did not look like her. I saw kids snickering. My Mom was clean, but her clothes were old and didn't fit well. I was embarrassed for her and for me." —Timothy

"Mom and Dad were not clean. There was no way to bathe. We were almost always camping because we were homeless. I did not want anyone to meet them." —Tammy

People in my research (Beegle, 2000) long to have the "right" clothing and shoes and be clean. They feel "abnormal" because of their appearance and their parents' appearance.

HOMES. Limited employment opportunities and poverty level incomes affect the stability of individuals' housing experiences. Inadequate housing is a theme that often emerges as one of the hardships of living in poverty, and one that is the biggest influence on the morale and stability of their lives. The family housing situation adds to their feelings of being ashamed and increases their perception that their family is "different" and that they do not fit in.

"I could never bring anyone home to our dump. I never wanted anyone to know it was my home." —Zach

"There were always extra people living at our house, It was always a mess and even if I wanted to bring someone home, there wasn't any room." —Larry

"I went to a friend's house once. She had bowls that matched. I always wanted bowls that weren't Golden Soft margarine containers." —Kathy

"We lived in a car most of the time, I tried so hard to hide that, but kids found out, and they could be vicious." —Megan

People in my research (Beegle, 2000) describe their efforts to make their homes nicer. They share stories of cleaning, building, and repairing the places where they live, but no matter how hard they try, most report that they remain "shamed" by their homes or by their lack of a home of their own.

In addition, the grim reality is that, more and more, the communities that are struggling with poverty are places where violence is rampant and hope for moving out of poverty is less and less likely.

AVAILABILITY AND QUALITY OF FOOD. Like housing, food is not only a necessity to people in poverty, but also gains additional importance by becoming a status symbol and indicator of their self worth. Most of the participants in my research (Beegle, 2000) share stories of how food is a barrier for them to belong and relate to others. They discuss not having the type of foods that other people are eating, which makes them feel inferior. Others share stories of not having food or having to purchase food with food stamps and the embarrassment that comes with that.

"I had cold pancake sandwiches for lunch. They were just awful. I just wanted what the other kids had." —Joyce

"My Mom packed me a sack lunch. She didn't have a quarter to buy me milk so she put tea in a mayonnaise jar. Once the tea leaked and when I got off the bus, the sack tore, the jar shattered. I just stood there and cried I was so embarrassed. I completely dreaded going to school. I wanted to be invisible."—Kathy

"I worried about my shoes and my lunch. Both always embarrassed me. It was such a thrill to have the treats that other kids had, like Twinkies."—Diane

"We got commodities, the powdered milk, peanut butter and stuff like that. I hated it. I could not understand what was wrong with our family. Why couldn't we go to the store and get milk in a jug like everyone else?"—Rob

People in generational poverty often go hungry. In my research, many share stories of hunger. They tell of feeling "weak" and "shaky" from not having enough food to eat.

"I remember many times we would go without food for days. We would get weak and to the point of not wanting to eat. My older sister would force something down us."—Billy

This level of hunger affects not only their feelings of self-worth, but also their health. The brain and cognitive abilities are also impaired by lack of nutrition. Most report that their families are,as a result of hunger, stress and lack of medical care,"sick all the time."

PARENTS' WORK. What the parents do to earn money also affect the self-esteem of people in poverty. The majority of the participants in my research report feeling that their personal worth is judged by the kind of work their parents do or do not do. They describe feelings of wanting their parents to have "normal" jobs.

"If your parents worked in the factory, that was a good thing. But if they worked in fast food or didn't go to work at all, everyone made fun of you."—Allen

"My dad drove an ice cream truck for short time, At first the kids thought it was cool. Then, after awhile they began to make fun of me and ask why my dad didn't get a real job."—Leroy

"My parents did migrant work and I just always wished they were normal like the parents on TV that go to clean jobs."—John

"Wanting to belong and be like everyone else" is a common phrase attached to the ends of stories of embarrassment related to poverty by all races. Freire (video taped speech at Santa Cruz University, 1989) discussed that what is normal in a society is determined by the middle-class through the media. People in poverty are not able to live up to the middle-class standards of food, jobs, housing, cars, clothing, and often-expected behavior (such as gift giving or completing outside-of-school projects). This sends powerful shaming messages that make them feel like outsiders and deeply affect their self-esteem and expectations.

LIFE OUT OF CONTROL. For those in generational poverty, their harsh living realities leave them feeling like they have no control over their lives. Their daily lives are a series of reactionary battles for survival with little, if any, opportunities to shape or choose their futures. For too many this comes with a strong feeling that something is personally wrong with them, and that there is nothing they can do to change it. People report that there is no point in planning ahead for the future because everything that happens in the context of poverty is out of their control.

> *"Life just happens. No one makes plans. When you are poor, it's like life has spun out of control and there is nothing you can do."—Joann*

As a result people in poverty often give up planning and spend their lives responding to what life throws their way. They feel there is little point in trying practice prevention.

HEALTH. People in generational poverty have little or no medical care. In my research (Beegle, 2000), most of the participants can not remember ever going to a doctor or knowing of anyone in their family who went to a doctor. The result is a lot of sickness and early deaths.

> *"Everyone in my family was always sick. We didn't have heat most of the time. We missed a lot of school because of sickness."—Kenneth*

> *"I can't think of a single time going to the doctor. If we were too bad off, we went to the emergency room."—Frank*

> *"I didn't know people went to the doctor. I thought everyone went to the emergency room."—Sherie*

> *"I never knew anyone who lived past 60. I thought that was normal."—Maria*

In addition to lack of medical care, they rarely have the money to purchase prescriptions. Often, if they get their prescriptions filled, they have to share these "precious" prescription medications—including antibiotics—with other family members and friends who badly need it too. Access to dental or vision care is even harder, and simply impossible in most cases.

"I never saw a dentist. Didn't even know you were supposed to until you needed false teeth."—David

"People in my family got their glasses from a second hand store. They would just go in and put some on and say, 'These will do.' No one had the money to go to a real eye doctor."—Vicki

Not having enough money to improve their health situations affects how people in poverty feel about themselves. Psychology tells us that human beings can gradually and incrementally grow used to anything: people in poverty grow used to their aches and pains, used to not being able to see, and become accustomed to looking at missing teeth in the mirror.

MONEY, AS A SOURCE OF CONTROL. In my study (Beegle, 2000), individuals from generational poverty report that not having the resources to get the basic necessities contribute to their feelings of "hopelessness." Most feel that without money, their lives are out of control, and they have no power to change their life situations. They associate money with safety, security, and choices for themselves and their families.

"If you have money, your problems don't seem as big. You can get help and solve them before everything is out of hand."—Phil

"Money can open doors. The doors may not be sealed, but they are hard to get into if you don't have money."—Larry

"People who have money have choices. It's harder without money. No one chooses to be without money. My parents worked hard. For 10 years, they made payments on a house thinking it was the ticket to security and then found out that the bank had no deed. They lost everything."—Julie

Money is also associated with power and control. Having money means more opportunities, ease of mind, and expanded choices. It means if something broke, you can get it fixed. Money, for many of the people in poverty, means being treated with respect and feeling like they are somebody (Beegle, 2000).

"I had a high school counselor who said college could help me make money. I wanted money because money meant control of your life. The counselor helped me with the paper work."—David

"I had a cousin who told me I could get money if I went to college. I knew money would give me power over my life."—Joseph

---

Not having money was often paralyzing for my research participants. They closed themselves off from the rest of society with dark curtains or hid out in bedrooms or basements. More isolation—more being cut off from possibility. They reported that their crisis often became worsened because of not having money. Overall, individuals from generational poverty feel money can improve their quality of life and their life chances, and many (77 percent) report feeling that without money they cannot dream or make choices, because, if they do dream, they would be let down or fail.

Concepts that Poverty Teaches

"Meanings are in people, rooted in their life experiences, not words!"

Daily life experiences and conditions create worldview and shapes priorities and meanings associated with people, roles, and concepts (such as, what does it mean to be a mom or to have a job?). Communicating and serving people in poverty situations requires an ability to create shared meaning and use examples and incentives that make sense to those experiencing poverty. What follows is a list of words and their meanings as defined by people who struggle with the daily hardships of poverty.

Fate—Life happens; we have no power to change it. All we can do is react to it.

Failure—Failure is inevitable. We have no hope for success, since there is no way to overcome what we feel to be our "inherent deficiencies."

Success— Since it is not clear what makes people succeed and since most people we know work very hard and are still struggling, we generally feel success is unattainable and limited to people who have a lot of luck.

Future—The future is unclear, unpredictable, difficult, and painful to envision; it is better to focus on living for now.

Job—A job means working long hours, but it does not pay a living wage nor provide enough money to pay the rent and buy food. It offers little or no respect. It takes us away from our family and you still go hungry. Individuals are hardly ever promoted.

Money—Money is to be used before it gets away, as there is never enough anyway.

Emotions—Emotions are to be expressed whenever they are felt—publicly and privately. They show that you are genuine.

Police—Police often hurt the people we love, therefore they act/feel like the "enemy": unfriendly, out to get us, and to be avoided.

Education—Education is useless. It is for other people, not us. It only takes us away from our family and causes additional stresses because we don't have the status symbols to belong (right knowledge, language, clothes, shoes, food, car, house, etc.).

Teachers—Teachers don't understand us. They also feel/look like the "enemy" to us. It seems as if they don't like people like us. They act as if we are invisible and make us feel unwanted, not cared about, and stupid because we don't know things that others seem to have mastered.

Healthcare—Healthcare is non-existent, or there is not enough healthcare coverage or access to preventive services. We have to wait too long to get help and only go to the emergency room if we are very sick. With no health coverage, prescription medicine and glasses are luxurious, and remedies need to be shared with family members and friends.

Doctors—Since doctors are only seen when family members are extremely ill, doctors become associated with being the bearers of bad news. If we stay away from them, they can't tell us bad news and won't owe them any money. Doctors are not seen as advocates or as caring individuals, but are seen as clinically distant and "knowing everything." The feeling is that they do not care about you. They only want money.

Dentist—The thought of dentists evoke feelings of fear...people we know don't go to the dentist, since they can never afford it. If lucky enough to access dental care, it's a tremendous hassle with a lot of "red tape" and then we experience a great deal of pain. Brushing and flossing are rules other people made up. They won't help us. Other things are more pressing than our teeth.

Nutrition and Exercise—Not words we use. Our worry is getting food on the table every night just to survive. Whatever is going to happen to our bodies will happen no matter what we do. Nutrition and exercise must have been created by and for people who have too much time and money on their hands.

Barriers to Success:
The Challenges of Living
in Poverty

People in poverty face many barriers that impede their efforts to experience success and have genuine life opportunities. These barriers can be grouped into two major categories: systemic barriers and internal barriers.

Systemic Barriers

Poverty forces people to deal with the many barriers that emanate from the structure of our social system. Many of these barriers are the result of the way institutions are currently organized, and stem from the values and perspectives that people in poverty adopt from the daily conditions they experience. These structures put people from generational poverty in many challenging positions where they see no levels of support or avenues of opportunity. In most cases, the fact that many of the barriers have systemic roots is invisible, even to people in poverty. The following are some of the systemic barriers encountered by people in poverty.

THE SILENCE ABOUT ISSUES OF POVERTY AND THE INVISIBLE NATURE OF SOCIAL CLASS

Social class is rarely used as a separate framework to analyze barriers to success. When social class is addressed in the United States, it is tightly linked to issues of race and racism. In fact, race is widely believed to be one of poverty's foundations. After the civil rights movement, many social service programs began to focus on eradicating racism and providing members of minority groups with fair and just opportunities for success. But poverty crosses race and ethnic barriers. It is true that proportionately, the numbers of people in poverty in minority populations is higher, but, of the 37 million people living in poverty in the Unites States, the majority are Whites (Census, 2005). For those in poverty who are White, resources and programs were and are scarce. For them, poverty also carries an additional stigma.

While the poverty among minorities is increasingly associated with unjust and inequitable conditions, White people are intensely blamed for their poverty. Most people in my study from poverty who are White reported feeling that their hunger, homelessness, and other poverty experiences were viewed as a result of bad choices they had made. There was little or no understanding that without education and skills they were highly unlikely to earn a living wage. In addition to their poverty being "their fault", many people in poverty who are White report that poverty-related barriers such as lack of basic education and work skills, and unstable living conditions were viewed as personal deficiencies rather than the result of a social structure that lacked basic support services. A majority of White people report feeling that their "Whiteness" led people to assume that they had privileged lives. Others assume that because they are "White," they should be able to "make it." Never mind if they were born into generations of homelessness and illiteracy. They are the one group of human beings in our society that we can and do call "trash."

"People assumed I was a White middle-class male and treated me like I've always had it good. I didn't have the energy to let them know what I'd been through."
—Joseph

"I had a teacher tell me to not participate in a class discussion because she wanted to hear from the females and the minorities. 'You White males always get to speak.' She had no clue that I came from the ghetto. I had never had a voice and no one ever listened to me."—Larry

"I needed financial help when I went to college. I needed tutors. There seem to be no help for anyone unless they were handicapped or a minority. I had to struggle alone."
—White female, 50s

"I knew early on that I did not fit in at school. People there assumed that I had experiences that I knew nothing about. They didn't know a thing about my life, but they thought they did because I was White and male. The only thing I might have in common with other students was a class assignment."—Rob

People in poverty who are White are the one group we can publicly humiliate. "White Trash" parties, posters, hats, cookbooks, and jokes are rampant. What does it do to a human to live in a society where it is OK to publicly call them trash? Freire says they will eventually own it and say things like "I am white trash and proud of it" What else can they do? Without targeting poverty as a societal problem that cuts across racial lines, the social class conditions for millions of Americans will remain invisible, and the barriers they face will remain unaddressed.

Stereotypes and lack of understanding: Most people in the United States, including those in poverty, have not had a chance to learn about poverty, its causes, and its history—since it is not part of the formal educational process in the Unites States (Loewen, 1995). Instead, the media increasingly influences our views, attitudes, and opinions about poverty and the people living in it—portraying them as lazy, drunk, oversexed, ignorant buffoons who continuously make bad choices.

This extreme stereotype has lead many people to believe that poverty is a result of bad choices or some personal "deficiency" in morals and character (such as laziness—people not working hard enough). Even though low pay is one of the major structural causes of poverty, rarely do we examine the earning potential for someone who is uneducated or unskilled in the United States.

Questioning the structural causes of poverty or pointing out the rigidity of the social class system is perceived to be a politically incorrect topic for public discourse. The voices of people who live in poverty situations are rarely heard, and their perspectives are rarely valued or included when policies and practices that directly affect their lives are created.

> *"I'm ashamed of my classism. I had no idea. I have been an anthropologist for 30 years and I never considered why people were poor beyond the stereotypes. I have judged and stereotyped people in poverty. I did not know until this training."*
> *—Beegle Conference Participant*

Unfortunately, most people in poverty report being misunderstood and unjustly pigeonholed by those with the power, position, and ability to help them the most. They report feeling judged, ridiculed, and condemned for their social-class experiences (including their language and middle-class knowledge gaps). People who make decisions about funding and services for people in poverty often have little or no understanding of the history of poverty in the United States or the structural causes of poverty, making it nearly impossible for them to suspend judgment and offer the kind of help needed to improve the conditions of those living in poverty. If a helping professional or person looking in on poverty has some type of poverty experience, they often assume that, because they made it out of poverty, the person being served should be able to do the same. Many people fail to examine the resources and privileges such as growing up with nutrition, stable housing and health care. Knowing someone who benefited from education and being connected to people who have succeeded in the labor market are privileges. Having people you connect to networks of support is also a privilege. These privileges would help people to make it out of poverty.

> *"It is offensive to me when people make comments about people who are poor. There is no recognition for the fact that my cousins are just as smart if not smarter than I am, work just as hard as I do, and are just as artistically creative, intelligent, and beautiful—but they don't have degrees! I don't want to be an example of the stereotype that says, 'If you just work hard, you can pull yourself up by the bootstraps.' That's just not true. My success is not because I worked harder than somebody else. Just as it's also not true that my best friends are in prison or dead because they weren't working hard enough. People are willing to work hard; there are just roadblocks over and over again."—Maria*

In order to have the self-esteem necessary to treat themselves as worthy of better circumstances, people in poverty need to understand that their living situations are due to circumstances created by a distressed society and not personal deficiencies. A majority of people from poverty report feeling empowered when they gained knowledge (through their education and interactions with others who had different social-class backgrounds) that allowed them to understand their cultural and poverty experiences. They reported feeling better about themselves and their families when they understood that they were not at fault or the cause of their poverty (Beegle, 2000). It is hard to feel hope and motivation if you believe you and those you love caused your poverty.

> *"Learning about class issues made me realize that there were clear structural reasons for the poverty and it wasn't mine or my family's fault."—Kathy*

> *"I was so excited when I learned about class. Finally, I had the language and knowledge to understand and help others understand that I wasn't deficient and neither was my family."—Leroy*

> *"I felt that my experiences growing up were validated for the first time when I learned about social class. I never realized it wasn't just my family or people from my race having these experiences."—Joseph*

Isolation and lack of social mobility: Despite the widespread belief that our society is a classless and open society where people can move freely and live wherever they want, the observed reality reflects a world divided, where people are confined to their respective social class, living in isolation within the boundaries of that class, and with the odds of escaping poverty getting smaller (Levine and Nidiffer, 1996).

In my research (Beegle, 2000), I found that people tend to interact with those belonging to their own social class: middle-class people interact with others who are middle-class, and people in poverty interact primarily with other like them. People living in poverty often report feelings that they do not "belong" or "fit in" outside their families and communities. People dress and behave differently than they do—eating different foods, driving cars that are not like theirs, and living in homes that are often very different than the ones in their neighborhoods. This isolation ensures that people in both groups rarely gain access to people who may have different ideas, experiences, or dreams, thus stereotypes are often perpetuated. There are few opportunities for meaningful interaction where empathy and understanding can occur.

Levine and Nidiffer (1996) reported that there is increased concentrations of people who are poor in both rural and urban areas resulting in fewer contacts with those who are not experiencing poverty. Wilson's (1987) research supported Levin and

Nidiffer's findings that people in poverty in the United States have become more isolated and the communities in which they reside increasingly poorer.

The dominant culture trains and educates helping professionals to maintain a clinical distance from people living in poverty as proof of their professionalism. They are taught not to get too close to the people they are working with—not to get personal or share personal stories. As a result, the only role models that a person from poverty comes in to meaningful contact with who has benefited from education or training and who are successful in the labor market are busy staying disconnected from them. This imposed isolation maintains the stereotypes and ensures little or no meaningful cross-class connections. It also prevents people from making meaningful connections that could truly impact their poverty experiences.

Institutional punitive structures: They are often left out because of lack of money. There are many structures in place that deny people in poverty the support they need by punishing them for things that are, most of the time, out of their control. For example:

• **Schools:** Students sometimes are not allowed to go to recess or participate in athletics for being tardy or for not completing their homework. They are also restricted because of high registration fees or equipment costs. How many people can be on time when they are in crises? What do you call homework when you don't have a home? Students are also locked out of activities because of fees or equipment cost. They do not get their school pictures or yearbooks which are an important part of their history.

• **Banks:** People living in poverty are often denied access to bank accounts (for reasons such as not being able to get proper identification or not having a permanent address). They often struggle with bad credit or no credit. They can pay 20 percent of their check at a commercial check-cashing service because they have no identification. Also, if one has $2000 in the bank, they get interest. If one only has $2, the bank may take it and close the account to cover service fees!

• **Local shopping:** Because they lack a bank account or credit, people living in poverty often pay more. Customers often pay ten times the amount of an item at a rent-to-own store than if it were purchased in a retail store. Because of lack of transportation, their choices may be limited. At local convenience stores—often the only places to shop in poorer neighborhoods—bread, milk, butter, and other staples cost considerably more than they do in larger grocery stores.

• **Loans**: Payday and title loan organizations charge up to 500 percent interest on loans. Middle-class people who need a short-term loan can often turn to family or have the credit necessary to borrow for emergencies at a much lower interest rate. People living in poverty may not have this as an option.

- **Drug-rehab centers:** When people in poverty who are addicted to alcohol or drugs look for help, the only help in many communities is often incarceration. If there is help, they are often told there is a wait list to get services. If they are fortunate enough to receive services, they generally receive five days of drug and alcohol rehabilitation even though to become drug or alcohol free requires a much more intensive program.

- **Prisons**: People living in poverty are over represented in prisons, most of the time for stealing (generally related to trying to meet basic needs) and crimes for self-medication or illicit trade. The majority of people in prison can not read beyond and 8th grade reading level.

  Mentally challenged individuals are incarcerated in many states because there are no monies for facilities or services for them. Youth who struggle with mental illness are placed in juvenile detention centers in 33 states due to lack of medical services for them.

- **Homeless camps**: People experiencing homelessness are continually being forced to move from where they are living, or they are threatened with arrest/arrested for such things as trespassing, vagrancy, and loitering. In Oregon, it is illegal to stay in a state campground unless you have a home address. It is also illegal to sleep on the streets in most cities in the U.S. Where can a person go if they are without a home?

- **Insurance agency:** If a person does not have money for automobile insurance, they often have to pay three times more than those who have consistently had car insurance. If they are stopped without insurance, they are required to file an SR22 form, which means they must maintain an equable amount of insurance coverage for a given period of time (three years in Oregon) or their license is automatically suspended. This requires hundreds of dollars that those in poverty usually can't afford. Their cars, often doubling as their homes, are towed and they are left stranded. We pass laws telling people they can not drive without car insurance—which completely ignores the reality that the U.S. Is a driving society. We do not have transportation systems to get people where they need to go when they need to be there. People in crisis of poverty are often forced to drive illegally because they have to get to work and they are often running from agency to agency trying to get crisis needs met.

We continue to ask students and families living in poverty to change their behavior. Most often, they are not in a context that allows them to change. Herbert Gans (1995) says that we keep asking people in poverty to "act" middle-class; thinking that by doing so, they will achieve the same successes. People in poverty do not have the luxury of the middle-class resources in order to do so. No matter how much we punish students who are homeless or in crisis for being late, the punishment will not help them be on time. Punishment will not help them to succeed if they are living in crisis with issues of hunger, evictions, cars being towed, lights be-ing shut off, etc. With all this crisis, it is likely that they will continue to be late! No matter how much we take away from the adults on public assistance, their situation (and their socialization that something is wrong with them) may not allow them to follow-through with what we are asking them to do. We cannot punish people out of their poverty. Talking down to them, judging them, or taking away resources will not work because it will not change the context in which they live nor im-prove the conditions under which they suffer. Just as Timothy Smeeding wrote in his article, *The Poverty Quagmire,* "Efforts that simply attempt to change the behavior of people living in poverty, and put the blame entirely on them, will fail. Working hard is simply not enough. The government needs to support people, not merely threaten them. Or else, 40 years from now, a future government will be threatening their children."

Fragmentation of available help: There are a multitude of agencies and educa-tional institutions available to serve people in poverty. Unfortunately, there is little collaboration among these agencies, making coordination difficult and the likeli-hood of "disconnections" in responding to people's needs very high. Many helping organizations will require people with a crisis to go to several organizations and get a little help from each to resolve the crisis. This division leads to the inefficiency of these agencies, as a whole, and becomes another factor in the creation of barriers to the self-sufficiency of those in poverty seeking institutional solutions to problems faced by those that are impoverished.

During my time in poverty, I often spent 90 percent of my time going from agency to agency to get $25 from each one to add up to the $150 needed to get my lights turned back on. Rarely do organizations combating poverty pay sufficient attention to how (or even if) all of the social service pieces fit together. The complexities are often bewildering to the service providers, and even more confusing and insur-mountable to those in need. Matching existing resource capacity and newly adopt-ed organizational programs to gaps in the service structure is rare. Service providers must recognize that the multi-dimensional nature of poverty requires a coordinated, multi-dimensional and unified response. We saw examples of this after Hurricane Katrina. Housing, employment, and health care workers all set up shop together to address the crisis. This collaboration of services provides a comprehensive ap-proach to helping people move out of poverty.

Most organizations set up to serve people in poverty, at best, help them "cope" with their poverty conditions, and rarely acknowledge their unmet needs for esteem and self-actualization. In many welfare to work programs, we teach people how to shake hands, how to fill out a resume, or how to interview. We fail to realize that many people in poverty have come to believe that they are not smart—that they have nothing to offer. We have to undo the strong messages sent in the United States that people in poverty are not smart, not as capable, and not as responsible as middle-class people. Services are rarely designed for or aimed at helping people move out of poverty or preparing them to be in a position to aspire. In addition, myths and stereotypes about poverty and those experiencing poverty continue to guide federal and state rules, regulations, policies, and funding. If we believe the myths and stereotypes, the attitude is "why should we help them?" Furthermore, some members of these organizations lack a comprehensive, non-judgmental understanding of the needs and worldview of people in poverty, something that makes their best-intended interventions reactionary and ineffective. If you are judging, you can not help.

The current fragmented reactionary approach to addressing the challenges of poverty not only falls short of helping people move out of poverty but also keeps our society from addressing and eradicating the root causes of poverty. A comprehensive approach is needed to truly move people forward. This all-inclusive approach to addressing poverty can only be achieved through partnerships among organizations and people that currently serve and interact with those in poverty: educational, social service, judiciary and law enforcement, and health care workers. Partnerships will give us power to build the capacity of those living in poverty conditions and to initiate structural changes that will alleviate some of the barriers they face. Business people, politicians and other organizations that may not have direct relationships to helping people move out of poverty must also step forward—to mentor, to contribute resources and to open the doors of possibility for those who have not had genuine opportunity.

Failure to reach out and communicate with people in poverty: People who grow up in poverty conditions without the benefit of a good education, often rely on "word of mouth" for their information. If the people you serve are verbal people and you mainly rely on written means of communication, your message will not get across to them. It will be very difficult for them to get your meaning or develop a clear understanding of what you are trying to communicate. Sending a letter, using professional jargon, or providing information on a website are not effective ways of communicating with people in poverty! Fundamentally, if you do not receive a response, it is not communication. Sometimes a response is not confirmation that there is understanding. In my research (Beegle, 2004), 68 percent of people in poverty reported that after meeting with a professional they did not know what they were supposed to do next. The misunderstandings result from using unfamiliar language and examples they could not relate to.

Internal Barriers

The systemic barriers that people in poverty face often manifest themselves in a deep lack of self-esteem and a strongly ingrained sense of despair. Faced with what they perceive as impregnable barriers, people in poverty find no one to blame for their failures but themselves. Even if they verbally blame others, to try and save face, they keep internalizing the poverty.

The predominance of misconceptions, stereotypes and punitive structures, combined with the harshness of their daily struggles for survival and the illusiveness of any kind of success, create experiences for people in poverty that often lead them to internalize the blame for their poverty situation. This blame creates internal barriers that lower their self-esteem, extinguish their dreams, and further limit their abilities to succeed. This in turn greatly affects their positive expectations for a future and impedes their hopes to lead a fulfilling and successful life.

Internalizing the blame: People who live in poverty in the Unites States have experiences that teach them that they are not as good as other people and that they somehow deserve what has happened to them. Because we do not teach about structural causes of poverty, people in poverty often think of themselves as somehow deficient and less than others who live in more affluent circumstances (Freire, 1970). Growing up in poverty often meant that they were ostracized for their appearance and shamed into believing that if they were born into poverty they had done something to get there. As a result, a natural reaction of people in poverty is to hide the signifiers of his and her humiliation and develop a tough exterior. Shame and poverty go hand in hand.

Many of the shaming messages come from the interaction of people in poverty with those who are not familiar with their life experiences. Helping professionals, for example, often fail to show the people they serve that they are talented, creative, and worthwhile and that they are just as smart and motivated as middle-class people. They also fail to project the belief that middle-class people are not better human beings, but rather they are people who have simply received better opportunities and support.

Another source of these messages is people who tend to blame the character of people in poverty when something goes wrong, but blame the situation when the same thing happens to them. Attribution Theory (Heider, 1958; Jones, et.al., 1972; and Weiner, 1986) assumes that people try to determine why people do what they do. A person seeking to understand why another person did something may attribute one or more motives to their behavior. Attribution Theory explains that people tend to attribute causes for behavior to the situation (or to factors outside themselves) when they understand and empathize with the circumstances of a situation. Alternately, a lack of understanding typically leads a person to place the cause of the misbehavior on the other person (or to their personality and other internal traits). For example, someone may say, "I got a ticket for speeding, but it was a speed trap." But when they hear of another person receiving a speeding ticket, they may say, "She is a speeder." Another example would be someone saying, "I was going through a rough time and started drinking too much. I put my family through a lot and needed help." But when describing another person's problem with alcohol, they might say, "He is an alcoholic and does not really care about his family."

Middle-class and wealthy people understand their own circumstances and attribute the causes of their behavior to the situation. However, they tend to attribute the behavior of people in poverty to the personalities of the people rather than the situation. Blaming someone's personality degrades the person and leaves no hope. It is not helpful since most people see personality as an essential, unchangeable quality. Attributing cause to a situation allows the option of identifying solutions to a problem through changing the situation.

COVERT INFERIORITY MESSAGES

When was the last time you had to visit your Department of Motor Vehicles for one of the services that couldn't be done in the express line, or get an updated copy of our social security card? If you live in a big city, these situations may call for you to take a number, wait in line for an hour or more, and experience frustration of not having the correct paperwork so that you need to come back at another time—so you can stand in line for another hour. These offices are generally open from 9-4, not convenient hours for those of us with jobs. For most of us, these "chores" happen infrequently and we endure them.

What would your life be like if most of the services you needed to survive required this kind of take-a-number-and-wait-your-turn, we're-sorry-you-are-not-properly-prepared experiences? Many of the messages we receive about our worth are not communicated directly through verbal communication, but come to us indirectly through nonverbal means, such as the amount of time we have to wait, the tone of voice in which we are addressed, or the look on someone's face as they see how we are dressed. When messages do not fit our self-concept, such as the long wait for the middle class person, we either dismiss them as an anomaly or find a way around the situation. However, if our daily life is full of similar types of messages, we tend to believe them and take them on as part of our self-concept. (Debra Hornibrook, 2006)

Society and its institutions repeatedly send the messages that people in poverty are "less than," through:

- Nonverbal negative reactions to the "others" whose behavior and appearance do not fit those of the middle class: reaction to clothes and appearance, language use such as improper grammar and ethnic vernacular, or home life

- Extremely long waits for any government-assisted health treatment or any assistance provision

- Jobs that pay less than living wages. A person may work two or three jobs and still not make a living wage sufficient to pay the monthly housing, utility, and food costs. Society's message is "work harder."

- Jobs in which employees are treated with very little respect and must often suffer humiliation in order to keep their jobs.

LIMITATIONS ON FUTURE PLANS AND DREAMS

The life experiences of people in poverty are defined by lack of access to support, understanding, and the perception and reality of limited possibilities for success.

Expectations for employment. Research shows that expectations for jobs and careers are directly linked to social class (Beegle, 2000, and Cookson & Persell, 1985). People in poverty have expectations for jobs that are strongly shaped by their parents and by others around them. When asked what they wanted to be when they grew up, they often answer that they do not have job or career goals. They also report that they never thought about "being something." Comments such as "I don't have any memory of wanting to be anything," "I had no dreams of what I wanted to be," and "I never had a 'to be' fantasy," are frequently reported by people from all races.

> *"I just wanted to survive and grow up. I never really thought about being anything. I never considered myself to be worthy to be anything."—Rueben*

> *"I had no specific career goals, No advice from parents, and high school counselors were a joke, and that's being kind. I wanted to have kids. I never pictured a husband, just babies. When I got a little older I thought maybe a vet because I loved animals. But I was told you have to go to school forever and it cost too much money."
> —Lorraine*

Many of the females in my research (Beegle, 2000) who identified a future goal wanted to be mothers, with a few males identifying parenting as their future goal as well. If you do not believe there are possibilities for you, your children often become your hope.

> *"I don't remember thinking of myself as being in a profession, I just assumed I would get married and be a mother. It was too scary to dream of anything else. That would mean planning for the future, something that was foreign to me."—Kimberly*

> *"I had no idea. I helped to raise my brothers and sisters, and assumed I'd have kids of my own."—Luke*

"I had no idea what I was going to be. I knew I wanted a wife, children, and a job to support them and my parents."—Eugene

When asked how they would earn a living, the majority of participants reported that they would find "some kind" of work. Sixty-nine percent of the participants had parents who were not in the labor force. They survived on welfare, disability, under the table work or migrant work. These participants talked about jobs as abstract concepts. They did not have a specific idea about what a job for them would be. Other participants described jobs with which they were familiar. This included: jobs they had seen performed in their communities (such as police officer, hair stylist, clerk, office worker, waitress, or truck driver); jobs that were held by people they knew (such as working in manufacturing, textiles, fishing, glass factory, cannery, sign painting, or seasonal migrant work); and jobs they had seen enacted or portrayed on television (such as a Solid Gold dancer, ballet dancer, nurse, or doctor).

"My Mom always said getting an office job would be good. You could stay clean and it would be glamorous."—Joann

The few students who identified professional career goals most often identified "teacher" or "nurse" as their career goal.

"When I first became aware that I was supposed to earn a living, there was no way I was going to do what my parents did. The only other role models I had were my two elementary teachers. Teaching became my natural goal."—Steve

"I had a school nurse who really cared about me. I told my counselor I wanted to be a nurse and she said "you won't be able to do all that math and science." —Taylor

Coming from generational poverty, most did not have and were never given the tools to create a future vision of what they wanted to be as adults. They were not exposed to professional career opportunities other than what existed within their communities, and most of the jobs they were acquainted with or introduced to did not require a college education. If some did get a glimpse of possibility, their dreams were often shut down.

Expectations for education. The educational level of the parents is strongly linked to the educational expectations for their children (Beegle, 2000, Coleman, 1998). In poverty, parents are rarely educated beyond high school, and the goal for most of their children is to do just a little better than their parents did. Educational expectations for people in poverty are rigidly defined by gender roles, with females expected to achieve little or no education while males are expected to complete high school (at most). Rarely are either sex encouraged to aspire to college (Beegle, 2000).

The meaning of education. Participants in my research (Beegle, 2000) were asked to reflect back on what education meant to them and their families. Almost all participants reported that education had little or no importance. They explained that classroom activities rarely related to "their real lives." Tiger and Fox further explained this in their book, The Imperial Man:

> "An educational system that teaches a child to survive in, and cope with, the ghetto where he lives is more successful as an educational system than one that fails to teach him to live securely and successfully in the disintegrated society of white suburbia with which he has no identification and to which he may not even aspire."

For most, education was just something they "did" and never knew why. Some of the most common reasons for going to school included, "it was the law," they "had to be there," and they "just went and never gave it a thought."

> *"Education was just some requirements that someone had made up. It had nothing to do with our life. We were struggling for survival and would be fortunate if we reached a certain age and were still here."—Tom*

> *"We went to school to eat, not to learn or get educated. I didn't even know what 'get educated' meant. I thought if I could work with my hands, I'd be fine."—Timothy*

The majority of the participants from all races reported that they had no direction and did not understand what they could do with an education. Even when they had good grades, education had no perceived impact on their lives, nor did it offer prospects for success in their context.

Education is also perceived as a major cause of stress for people in poverty. In my research, most of the participants pointed out that education was not a positive force; rather it represented more problems in their already troubled lives. Across race, it constituted a source of discomfort, unhappiness, and stress. All participants shared feelings of "not belonging in school" and "wanting to stay home where they belonged" (Beegle, 2000).

> *"Education was stress to my family. I didn't do well even though I was smart. Getting all the things we needed for school and getting there every day was more pressure in our lives. I was headed toward drugs and a life of crime."—Leroy*

"School projects and homework were a joke. People like me never got school activities done. We either didn't know what we were doing and there was no one to help or we didn't have the right stuff to do a project and life was so chaotic anyway. We just didn't participate."—Carolyn

"I hated school holiday parties and gift exchanges. I would look desperately through my things trying to find something I could give that didn't look too used. I just wanted to be like everyone else."—Vicki

"The school and the teacher did everything right, but my mom and I were going hungry and being evicted. I needed to be with her, NOT in a classroom."—Lisa

People in poverty often report feeling like they do not "fit in" or do not "feel comfortable" in the educational environment. The underlying reasons for discomfort and not fitting in related to their poverty and poverty-related conditions such as not having money for school lunches (many participants refused to eat the "free" lunches because of the stigma attached); not having the "right" clothing; not living in the "right" house; and not riding in a "decent" car. Participants nodded and shared knowing smiles when remembering "hiding on the floor" of the car so no one could see the car they arrived in (Beegle, 2000).

Communication about the value of education. Communication about education in the home lives of people in poverty was limited. My study (Beegle, 2000) found that most (96 percent) recalled that their families did not talk about education. Statements such as: "There was no discussion at home"; "No one ever asked, 'How are you doing in school?'"; "There was no involvement"; "We never discussed grades"; and "We didn't talk about it at all" were the most common responses concerning communication about education. Participants reported that not communicating about education in their homes sent messages that it was not important and no one cared about it. When asked what was important and talked about, all participants agreed that daily struggles with poverty were the focus of their lives, and not "educational" or school-related issues.

"My parents were not educated. My mom couldn't even write her name. They were embarrassed about it and ashamed. They never talked about what was going on with me and school."—Vicki

"Education was fear. Fear they would take the kids away. People are trying to deal with basic needs. They don't have time to deal with kid's education or filling out papers at some agency."—Leroy

"Education was important in my home, but it could not compete with the realities of poverty"—Joyce

"Education was important. My mom would have liked us to get educated, but education was not as strong of a need as getting food for that day or finding a place to sleep."—Julie

Across lines of race and ethnicity, friends played a role in shaping what education meant. Ninety-seven percent of the participants in my study (Beegle, 2000) recalled that their friends shared many of their beliefs about education. Some participants shared how peer-pressure to "not gain an education" was especially difficult. They needed and wanted to belong and fit in with their friends. Friendships were an unseen, internal barrier to education. Gaining an education meant becoming an outsider, and they did not want to become outsiders to their friends.

"There was an unspoken agreement that no one should get any smarter than others in the neighborhood. There wasn't challenge or ambition and most of us were stereotyped into technical schools."—Tom

"I was friends with people like me. Those kids who thought education was important were from another world. We did not hang out with them."—Rob

"I never associated studying with success. I just thought intelligent kids did well and others like me and my friends didn't."—Joyce

Educational goals. The parents of my research participants were not educated beyond high school and most did not have a frame of reference or language to discuss education goals beyond their experiences. Many of my middle-class friends report tat for the, "going to college was like blinking." For students in poverty, going to college is like touching the moon- not a possibility. It's not something they would ever be able to do even if they dreamed it.

"My goal was to just get through high school. The goal is to do better than your parents, nothing more. Education meant nothing. I went to meet the boys, nothing more."—Kathy

"My Mom hoped all her kids would get a high school education. That was the great expectation. She said we could get jobs better than McDonald's if we finished high school."—Rob

"For my family, the 8th grade would be a great accomplishment. No one went beyond that. You needed to go to work at that point."—Leroy

"I could not imagine finishing high school and, if I did, it would be an incredible accomplishment because no one I knew went beyond the eighth grade."—Julie

"My dad thought high school was important. I got pregnant at 16 and at 17, then I finished high school for my dad."—Joann

"No one I knew believed education would make a difference for people like us. They just shoved us   through the system and didn't quite know what to do with us." —Joseph

How far a participant was expected to go with his or her education was also affected by gender. Educational expectations for people in poverty were rigidly defined by gender roles for both older and younger participants. My research on sex roles and social class (Beegle, 1992) showed sex roles grew more rigid in lower class families. The expectations for females from their families were that they would achieve little or no education. For all males in my study, the family expectations were that they would complete up to 10th grade or, at most, finish high school. Typically, neither sex reported being encouraged early on to aspire to a college degree (Beegle, 2000), with most being told education was "for the boys," and the girls were expected to "get married."

"Education up to high school was important for the boys but not the girls in my family. We were taken out of school a lot to work."—Joyce

"There are five girls in my family and one boy. We rarely went to school. My Dad said school was a social thing, and, besides, girls get married; they don't need school." —Tammy

"I was taught education was for the boys and marriage was for the girls. Why would anyone need education beyond [high school]?"—Larry

Summarily, the meaning of education for people in poverty is shaped by societal messages that people in poverty are not as smart and can't be educated by the context of poverty. Attitudes, values, and beliefs concerning education are formed based on the communication and experiences of people around them, including their families and friends. Most could not articulate why they went to school as children and teenagers, except that it was "something you did." Communication about education was rare in poverty-stricken homes. Messages that education was not important and not for "people like" them dominated the conversations. What was discussed most often were issues and feelings related to their struggle for survival and basic needs. A dominant feeling of not belonging characterized their schooling.

Changing the meaning of education to make it purposeful and relevant to people living in poverty requires learning about what they have passion and motivation for. For many, a strong motivator and passion is the desire to stop the poverty-related suffering of the people they love. It requires showing students and families in poverty how education can truly help them to move out of poverty.

Characteristics and Strengths of People in Poverty

Walter J. Ong, the author of *Orality and Literacy: The Technologizing of the Word* (1982), was the first to connect oral culture learning with and communication styles with poverty experiences. Ong found the conditions of poverty often created a need for people to get their information word of mouth and for them to live in the moment. In other words, they tend to get most of their information from other people or through word of mouth. The context of poverty and the style of receiving information shapes learning style, thought process, communication, and interactions. Every human being is born oral culture. A person learns a more middle-class print culture style of communication and learning if as a child they are surrounded by people who read for their primary information. Both oral and print culture characteristics are more fully explained in the Understanding and Communicating: Oral and Print Culture section of chapter two. Ong identified the main characteristics of oral culture learning and communication style as being present-oriented, relationship-based, spontaneous, holistic, emotional, physical and repetitious. These characteristics impact education, relationships, and work experiences for people in poverty.

- **Relationship based:** People who primarily rely on oral communication are relationship-based because they get their information from others. When they need information, they ask those around them with whom they identify. Relationships are at the heart of everything they do and are always their first priority—they are more important than anything else.

- **Spontaneous:** People who primarily rely on oral communication have a strong desire for variety. They have great abilities to "go with the flow" or jump from subject to subject with ease, bouncing from idea to idea, which is the nature of verbal communication. It is normal to interrupt and to have multiple conversations at once. Interrupting is seen as adding information and as a reflection of their interest in the conversation and the person speaking. They can focus on one idea, but prefer to go with the flow and consider—and voice—any ideas that come to mind.

- **Holistic:** Much of the meaning is in gestures, tone and the context in which they are communicating and relating. They tend to keep track of appointments by what is happening around them or what is on television, not by a clock.

- **Emotional:** People who primarily rely on oral communication are comfortable with emotions. There is emotion in your voice. Print does not have emotion. Oral culture people show emotions and feelings readily in most situations and are open to self-disclosing private details. Sharing their personal experiences and stories is their way of connecting with others. They also look for emotion, gestures and facial expressions from those they relate with as an indicator of caring and connection. They also look for emotion, gestures and facial expressions from those they relate with as an indicator of caring and connection.

- **Agonistic:** People who primarily rely on oral communication are quite physical. Using their body is an important part of how they relate and communicate with people. For them touch is a big part of how they learn and communicate-a pat on the shoulder-or a touch on the arm while talking is common. They also respond more physically and immediately to what is going on around them. They succeed most often when they are allowed and encouraged to touch and try what it is they are learning.

- **Repetitious:** Repeating the same thing over and over is a normal component of communication for people from oral culture. It is important for maintaining knowledge. Telling the same story over and over helps them in their understanding and with moving information from short-term memory to long-term memory.

- **Present oriented:** People who primarily rely on oral culture learning and communication style are highly in tune with the here-and-now. They focus on what is going on around them right now and are rarely interested in planning for the future. Poverty teaches a present orientation. The focus is on where you will sleep or what you will eat tonight. As soon as a word is spoken, it is gone. This teaches the oral culture person to be present in order to get information. Poverty also teaches a present orientation. Life is focused on immediate needs of food, shelter and other poverty-related crisis. Planning or focusing on the future is often hopeless because of the lack of resources to carry out plans and the belief that the future is grim.

Oral culture is not limited to or exclusive to those in poverty. People from many different racial and ethnic backgrounds relied more heavily on verbal communication than reading for living their lives and therefore often display a more "oral culture" style of learning and communicating. Women in America were educated much later than men and often display a preference for oral culture communication and learning styles. However, Ong found in poverty, regardless of race or sex, people worldwide displayed a more oral culture style of learning and communicating. Gender is another variable that shapes how people seek information. Ong (1982) found women tend to exhibit more oral culture characteristics than men since women came to rely on print as a source of gaining information later than men (largely due to the lack of education for women historically). However, Ong's research shows that with poverty, oral culture was the dominant learning and communicating style for both men and women across race and culture differences.

Ong (1982) also found that the context of poverty heightens the need for characteristics associated with oral culture. For example, in oral culture, people get their information from others they trust. They need relationships in order to get information and therefore place a high value on those relationships. In poverty, people seldom have possessions for any length of time. They may gain a TV or stereo, but may soon lose it (it may be taken as collateral, stolen, or sold for basic needs). Thus, the lack of possessions creates a high value in the people around them. Their children become their wealth. They may not like what a family member is doing and may say so. But if an outsider says anything bad about their family, they become extremely defensive and protective. Their world view is that relationships are all they have.

People from poverty are proud of certain values they hold (relationships as a priority, loyalty, lack of materialistic focus, and pride in their ingenuity and resourcefulness) and rightly so. They are people who are able to smile and find ways to have fun even when their world is often crumbling around them. These are just some of the many qualities yet to be discovered and valued by society.

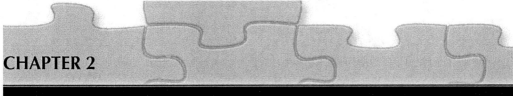

CHAPTER 2

SERVING PEOPLE FROM POVERTY

THE STARFISH

Once upon a time there was a wise man who used to go to the ocean to do his writing. He had a habit of walking on the beach before he began his work. One day he was walking along the shore. As he looked down the beach, he saw a human figure moving like a dancer. He smiled to himself to think of someone who would dance to the day.

So he began to walk faster to catch up. As he got closer, he saw that it was a young man and the young man wasn't dancing, but instead he was reaching down to the shore, picking up something and very gently throwing it into the ocean.

As he got closer he called out, "Good morning! What are you doing?"

The young man paused, looked up and replied, "Throwing starfish in the ocean."

"I guess I should have asked, why are you throwing starfish in the ocean?"

"The sun is up and the tide is going out. And if I don't throw them in they'll die."

"But, young man, don't you realize that there are miles and miles of beach and starfish all along it. You can't possibly make a difference!"

The young man listened politely. Then bent down, picked up another starfish and threw it into the sea, past the breaking waves and said—

"It made a difference for that one."

—Source Unknown

The Building Blocks for Serving People From Poverty

"There are among us children who sleep in hunger, rise in cold and live in ignorance, and they are of every color and every tribe. We ought not find their suffering easier to accept because they are not like us. We ought to realize that the dignity of all is the concern of all." (Pitts, 2006)

Understanding poverty and getting an insight on the world of people living in it should be the first building blocks in our attempts to serve people in poverty. Helping professionals and caring citizens can use the information presented in this book to validate work they are currently doing; to advocate and be a voice for shattering myths and stereotypes; and to eradicate systemic and internal barriers to moving out of poverty.

Shattering the myths about poverty and those who are poor and understanding the harsh reality of their lives are fundamental steps towards changing attitudes towards people in poverty and changing assumptions as we interpret their behaviors. Historically and currently, the dominant views about poverty causes and the people who live in poverty lead us toward "blaming" people for their conditions. We keep asking people to change, work harder, and succeed without any genuine attempt on our part to understand their context and the nature of the barriers it created which keeps them from advancing. We also offer a fragmented approach to solving poverty problems often focusing on the symptoms rather than on addressing the structural/root causes of poverty. The agencies, organizations, and individuals currently involved in helping people in poverty often work in isolation of one another. A coordinated, comprehensive approach is rare. As a society, we need to regain our focus and remember that it is our collective responsibility to eradicate poverty and make sure that no one suffers it atrocious conditions. We kept asking people to change, work harder, and succeed without any genuine attempt on our part to understand their context and the nature of the barriers it created which keeps them from advancing. We also became absorbed too often with fragmented problem solving, narrowly focusing on the "symptoms" rather than on addressing the structural/root causes of poverty. The agencies, organizations, and individuals currently involved in helping people in poverty function in total isolation. They lack a strategy to mobilize services and capitalize on available resources. As a society, we need to regain our focus and remember that it is our collective responsibility to eradicate poverty and make sure that no one suffers its atrocious conditions.

This section lays out the foundation for serving people in poverty and is based on the following assumptions:

- The main goals for helping people out of poverty are to help them see possibilities for success, believe in their worth, and recognize that they have something to offer.

- People in poverty have unique strengths and characteristics from living in survival mode.

- Understanding the learning and communication styles of people in poverty is key to success in serving them.

- Mentorship and building meaningful relationships between service providers and those they serve should be the basic organizing principle for any intervention or change program aimed at people in poverty.

- It is everyone's responsibility to reach out to people in poverty and become "ready" to serve them. We need to listen to their stories, learn about their strengths, and welcome their perspectives and suggestions before planning interventions.

- To ensure the effectiveness of our services we need to constantly ask the following questions:

  - Does the intervention I am suggesting or implementing make sense in their current context?

  - Am I preparing the people that I work with for success?

  - Am I considering their situation, resources, and health before asking them to follow through with my organization's programs or policies?

  - Are there supports that I need to build in and connect people to that will increase their ability to be successful?

If we ask these questions and respond accordingly, people's ability to move forward will dramatically improve.

Theoretical Foundation and Implications for Action

There are a number of theories and perspectives that provide us with the building blocks for a new paradigm to understand poverty and lay the foundations for action and change. All these theories focus on the premise that poverty experiences generate inherent strengths—thus the best way to serve them is to identify, believe, and build on those strengths. These theories include: Strengths Perspective, Resiliency Theory, Asset Theory, Relationship Development Theory, Identification Theory, and Social Capital Theory. Along with a brief explanation of each theory are guidelines for action to use when serving people from poverty.

Strength's Perspective

The strength's perspective underlies all other theories in this chapter providing the foundational assumptions for understanding poverty and serving people struggling in it. It is a distinctive lens for examining how we serve people living in poverty. Saleebey (1997) distinguished between the strengths perspective and resiliency; asserting that the strengths perspective is "an organizing construct that embraces a set of assumptions and attributes." It provides a way of thinking about people's behavior, events and interactions. Resilience is "an attribute that epitomizes and operationalizes what the strengths perspective is all about."

The strength's perspective approach is based on recognizing and focusing on the strengths that each person brings and developing individual success plans to build on those strengths. It proposes that every person should be treated as if her or his potential is unknown. The core ideas of the strengths perspective are empowerment, membership, regeneration and healing within two-way dialogue and collaboration. According to Saleebey, the philosophical underpinnings of the strengths perspective include five primary principles:

- Every individual, group, family, and community has strengths. In order to learn what these strengths are, one must listen to stories, narratives, and personal accounts.

- There must be recognition that life's difficulties and challenges may be injurious, but they can also be viewed as sources of creating strong survivors who can apply their survival skills, given genuine opportunity, to moving forward.

- Dreams, aspirations, and desires must be respected even if they appear to be set too high. It must be assumed that the upper limits of capacity are not known.

- A "helper" is best defined as a "collaborator" or "consultant," not an "expert," or "professional." The wisdom and resources of all parties concerned must be respected and acknowledged through listening to stories, fears, hopes, and dreams.

- Every environment is full of resources. Much of the energy, talents, ideas, and tools in individuals and communities are disregarded.

The strengths perspective principles can be used as a guide for framing services and learning that truly makes a difference for people in poverty. Find what is good about those you work with and start there. Most people from my research report not being able to recall a person who was successful in education or a career who ever said anything about their talents and strengths. People reported that the focus of their interactions with helping professionals was on what they "didn't know," "couldn't do," what they were doing wrong, or their not complying with a rule or policy such as being late, not having the right paperwork, etc.

When helping professionals focus on what is positive, good and right about those they serve, they see potential and those in poverty feel empowered. Find out what is good about those you teach or work with and start there.

Asset Theory

In *Building Communities from the Inside Out: A Path Toward Finding and Mobilizing a Community's Assets* (1993), Kretzmann and McKnight write about a strategy they called "asset-based community development." They created this strategy to address the inadequacies of the needs-driven deficiency model of dealing with the problems of residents living in troubled neighborhoods.

Their research found that the solutions provided by these deficiency-oriented policies and programs actually taught people that their well-being depended upon being a "client" and seeing themselves as people with special needs that could only be met by outside experts. They began thinking of "themselves and their neighbors as fundamentally deficient, victims incapable of taking charge of their lives and of their community's future" (Kretzmann and McKnight, 1993).

Kretzmann and McKnight found historic evidence indicating that significant community development only takes place when local people commit to investing themselves and their resources into the effort, so they proposed an alternative approach with activities and policies based upon the capabilities, skills, and assets of lower income people and their neighborhoods. They believed that once a community "mapped" its unique combination of gifts, skills, and abilities, they would discover a vast array of talents and skills that could be harnessed to multiply their own power and effectiveness to better solve their own problems and meet their own needs.

Researchers from the Search Institute further studied the notion of assets to see how personal assets related to growth and development. Their studies revealed strong and consistent relationships between the number of assets or resources present in a person's life and the degree to which she or he develops in positive and healthful ways. Results showed that the greater the numbers of assets experienced by a person, the more positive and successful his or her development would be. The fewer the number of assets present, the greater the possibility he or she would engage in risky behaviors.

I experienced this when staff at the displaced homemaker program asked me, "What kinds of things have you done?" I did not believe I had done anything worthwhile. I did not think I had any skills. My reply was, "I ain't done nothing." They began helping me to explore what personal assets I had by doing a personal inventory. My assignment was to write down everything I had done to earn money and every task that I did in my daily life. Staff took my list and began showing me that, in fact, I had a lot of assets. They said, "Look Donna, you have taken care of your kids, that means you have done daycare. When you had money, you have managed it, you have been an accountant." All the things I thought were "nothing," they showed me how people in the professional world did similar tasks and got paid for it. This increased my sense of self and my belief that I had some assets. I had something to offer. This gave me what Freire states is missing for people in poverty in America—HOPE!

In 1990, the Search Institute created a framework of 30 Developmental Assets (revised to 40 Developmental Assets in 1996) to describe the assets that young people must have in order to be successful. They divided the assets into two types (external and internal) and seven basic categories (caring support, empowerment and valuing, boundaries and expectations, constructive use of time, commitment to learning, social competencies, and positive identity).

The first 20 Developmental Assets focus on positive experiences that young people receive from the people and institutions in their lives. The four categories of external assets included in their framework are:

- **Support:** Young people need support, care, and love from their families, neighbors, and many others. They need organizations and institutions that provide positive, supportive environments.

- **Empowerment:** Young people need to be valued by their community and have opportunities to contribute to others. For this to occur, they must be safe and feel secure.

- **Boundaries and expectations:** Young people need to know what is expected of them and whether activities and behaviors are "in bounds" and "out of bounds."

- **Constructive use of time:** Young people need constructive, enriching opportunities for growth through creative activities, youth programs, etc.

The second 20 Developmental Assets focus on the internal qualities youth must possess in order to make responsible decisions about their present and their future. Caring adults must make a strong commitment to nurturing the internal qualities that guide positive choices and foster a sense of confidence, passion, and purpose. The four categories of internal assets include:

- **Commitment to learning:** Young people need to develop a lifelong commitment to education and learning.

- **Positive values:** Young people need to develop strong values that guide their choices.

- **Social competencies:** Young people need skills and competencies that equip them to make positive choices, to build relationships, and to succeed in life.

- **Positive identity:** Young people need a strong sense of their own power, purpose, worth, and promise.

The complete list of the 40 Developmental Assets for the different age groups (infants, toddlers, preschoolers, elementary age, middle childhood, and adolescents) can be found at www.search-institute.org/assets/assetlists.html.

Every person and every community has assets. It is important to first look at their strengths, resources, and assets, as well as help them define those they see within themselves. Once defined, we need to help promote the assets they currently have in their lives as well as work with them on developing those they do not possess. Asset theory has also found that it is important to include people in the decision-making processes that are used to create a plan of action for their futures—guiding them in ways that help them assemble their strengths into new combinations, and look for new opportunities and new sources of income—giving them more control over their lives and helping them see new possibilities for their future. This is the philosophical foundation for the approach that Communication Across Barriers adapts in the process of change that is further outlined in Chapter 3.

Resiliency Theory

Resiliency theory is commonly used in research that is concerned with understanding how people are able to overcome extreme barriers and find success (Bernard, 1994; McLaughlin, Irby, & Langman, 1994). There are many common definitions of resiliency in the literature.

Overall, resiliency is defined as the process of coping with disruptive, stressful, or challenging life events in a way that provides the individual with additional protective and coping skills than they had prior to the disruption (Richardson, 1986). This model places emphasis on an individual's ability to cope prior to disruptive events and develop new coping abilities resulting from the disruption. Other theories add new dimensions to our understanding of resiliency. Higgins (1994) described resiliency as "the process of self-righting and growth." This model suggests that as disruption occurs, the person affected will not only "cope," but manage to find a balance between the disruption and positive individual strengths, events, or people in his or her life. This process results in the person having gained additional coping skills. Similarly, Wolin and Wolin (1993) described resiliency as "the capacity to bounce back, to withstand hardship, and to repair yourself." All three definitions have to do with having the capacity to meet challenges and become more able as a result of the challenge.

Early studies on resiliency focused on individual characteristics and traits. They helped generate a list of characteristics that became associated with being resilient. Sheehy (1986) identified four characteristics of resiliency as well: 1) the ability to bend according to circumstances, 2) self-trust, 3) social ease, and 4) an understanding that one's plight was not unique. After a 50-year longitudinal study on men whose childhood was considered severely at-risk, Vaillant (1993) added the following characteristics of resiliency: resourcefulness, humor, empathy, worry, and the ability to plan realistically. Similarly, Higgins (1994) found three characteristics common among resilient individuals: a positive attitude; ability to confront problems and take charge of their own lives; and faith, which gave meaning to their lives. In her profile of a resilient child, Benard (1994) provided a profile that includes characteristics of social competence (responsiveness, flexibility, empathy, communication skills, a sense of humor, and any other pro-social behavior), problem solving skills (abstract thought, reflection, and ability to find alternatives for cognitive and social problems), autonomy (sense of identity, abilities to act independently, and to exert control over one's life) and a sense of purpose and future.

Saleebey (1997) recognized common individual characteristics, but like Benard, he asserted that resilience is not an inborn attribute. He advanced the notion that resiliency results from interactions within a particular context and the significance of resilience is most helpful when examined within a social context:

Further understanding of [resilience] is enriched by listening closely to the [person's] definition of what life has been and is all about: by regard for apparent potentials, expectations, visions, hopes and desires: by the meanings one gives to or finds in his or her circumstances, and not the least, the quality and extent of relationships.

The growing body of inquiry and practice in the area of resiliency acknowledges the importance of examining social context (Benard, 1994; Jordan, 1992; Saleebey, 1997). Researchers are becoming more and more clear that the extent to which characteristics of resiliency are present is directly related to the existence of internal and external protective factors (Saleebey, 1997). This more complex understanding of resiliency resulted in more attention given to the aspects of various institutions that foster resiliency.

Krovetz (1999) examined aspects of educational institutions that develop and support resiliency qualities especially in the areas of school culture and curriculum. Krovetz described particular aspects of school culture that foster resiliency. These are caring attitudes, high expectations, purposeful support, and meaningful student participation. Schools with these attributes emphasized the following: a sense of belonging for students, an emphasis on cooperation and celebrating successes, and the importance of leaders spending positive time with staff and students. Characteristics of the school curriculum that fostered resiliency were meaningful work, work that respects multicultural student perspectives, and using student input in curriculum, instruction, and assessment.

Resiliency theorists assert that resiliency is a process and an effect of connection (Saleebey, 1997). Individuals do not operate in a vacuum. The research findings on resiliency call for development of environments that challenge, support, and provide protective factors enabling people to develop characteristics that see them through difficulties.

The initial research on resiliency implied that one was either born with resiliency characteristics or had no chance to become resilient. As the theory developed, researchers came to realize that resiliency, or the ability to bounce back in the face of challenges, was directly impacted by the environment. In studying resilient children and their families, researchers have begun to identify important features that seem to give protection against the poor outcomes usually associated with living in environments with many risk factors. These so-called "protective factors" safeguard individuals in spite of difficult obstacles. Studies also show that the greater the number of protective factors a person possesses, the greater number of risk factors he or she is able to overcome. The protective factors seem to fall into three general categories: the qualities developed in the individual, the opportunities for support for their entire family, and the connections and support from outside the family.

Promoting resiliency can be accomplished by:

1. Helping individuals feel special or unique. Poverty in the United States teaches you that you are not someone with value and that you do not belong. People living in the environment of poverty need to know that there are good things about them. They need to know that they are not another problem for you to deal with.

2. Recognizing and valuing the strengths of an individual's family and friends. People from helping professions will often take an interest in an individual student or person that they are working with, yet they sometimes ignore or negatively judge that individual's family members. A person's sense of self is highly related to their family. Resiliency can only be built when there is trust. Valuing the people they care about builds trust.

3. Helping individuals see their opportunities. Find ways to brag about their strengths. Link their strengths to talents needed for success.

The majority of those in my study (Beegle, 2000) who were able to complete a bachelor's degree were treated special as a child by someone in their lives. Because they were singled out and given personal encouragement, they perceived that they were somehow different from others who were living in poverty. This feeling of being "different" helped them gain some confidence to try new things. In addition, the acquired belief that they were not like the others in poverty, helped them to be more open to people who were not from poverty backgrounds. Environment and interactions with others matter.

> *My cousin always told me I was smart and beautiful and that I could do anything. I believed her and was the first in my family out of six kids to go to college.*
> *—White female, 20s*

> *My Dad said I was his "good boy." My brother never went anywhere with his life. My Dad always told me I was the one who could do anything.—Black male, 40s*

Some participants (62 percent) reported that being recognized for their athletic, musical, or academic talents played a major role in persisting toward achieving a college drgree. Encountering people who felt they were smart and talented gave them the emotional support and practical guidance to have small successes. These small successes, motivated them to risk stepping outside of their comfort zone to become educated.

> *My co-worker said I should try college. She thought I was smart.—White female, 40s*

I had an employer who told me I was smart and I should go to college. I had never considered it before that.—White female, 50s

"I was good at football so my coach helped me connect with teachers who gave me extra academic support to catch up. That's how I made it."—Hispanic male, 30s

People in poverty rarely cite a program as the reason they were resilient enough to break poverty barriers. They always tell stories of a person or people who reached out to them. Positive relationships build resiliency and promote the ability of people in poverty to break out of poverty's iron cage.

Putting Relationships First

Much of the current literature on helping people move out of poverty suggests the necessity of building strong relationships (Burke, 1969; Knapp, 1984). These relationships need to be based on identification (Burke, 1969)—meaning that the person living in poverty and the helping professional see how they are like one another—to reach the bonding level and make a difference in the life of people in poverty. In their book, *The Imperial Man,* Tiger and Fox linked this type of relationship with learning:

> Humans "have been wired to learn in security, in familiar surroundings, from peers who will be lifelong companions and from elders who must be followed first and cared for later.' Humans are wired "to learn with an expectation of continuity in personnel and relevance of what is learned to what is done."

Outlined below is the Identification Theory as outlined by Kenneth Burke (1969), followed by the theory of relationship development by Mark Knapp (1984) with modifications to consider when working with people living in poverty.

Identification Theory

Kenneth Burke's (1990) Identification Theory points out that relationship building needs to be based on the principle of finding common ground. Human beings tend to seek out and accept information for how to live their lives from someone they trust and identify with. For people in poverty to learn new information, new ways of thinking and behaving, they need identification with someone who is making it. Someone who is practicing the new behavior and providing encouragement that they also can do it (get educated, trained, etc.).

Burke contends that the need to identify arises out of division; humans are born and exist as biologically separate beings and therefore seek to identify, through communication with people who are "like" them in order to overcome separateness. Maslow (1948) would call this need to belong. Identification requires being open to seeing the other person's perspective. Burke believes that when you identify with someone, it is like a symbolic rebirth: I can see through your eyes why you believe and value what you do. To identify with someone and find common ground, people

---

must self-disclose information about who they are and their experiences. There are multiple levels of self-disclosure, but for our purposes we will consider three:

Level 1—Sharing information regarding specific subject matter or resource

Level 2—Sharing personal stories, experiences, feelings and preferences

Level 3—Deeply personal information, gut-level values, and beliefs

Level 1: Unfortunately, most helping professionals interact and communicate with people in poverty at a sharing information level 1. For example, you have information about a resource, so you relay this information to the person needing help. This does not build connection. It does not say anything about who you are. At this level of self-disclosure, the person does not learn anything about you as a real person. They may be reluctant to accept or follow through on the information you are sharing and interpret that as "not possible for people like them," or "too far out of their comfort zone." Building identification helps people see that you are like them, that you learned the information or went through the program and you believe that they can too. At the sharing information level of self-disclosure, you, the helping professional, remain "other." This causes a struggle to be heard and difficulty in gaining commitment and follow-through.

> Example: At a recent training, a teacher commented to me that while she was grocery shopping one day she encountered one of her students who lived in poverty. The teacher said that she made an extra effort to go say "hi" to her student. The student surprised her by saying, "You shop?" The student did not identify with the teacher and could not imagine that the teacher did something that he was doing.

Level 2: Level 2 of self-disclosure promotes identification. It requires that you move beyond sharing formal, impersonal information to using personal examples. For instance, you could tell a student how you learned the subject you are teaching or how you used the information. It can be really powerful for people from poverty backgrounds to hear that a professional had to learn the information in some way. This society often teaches that the people who are successful in life already know information just because they are smarter. People living in poverty need to know that the professionals they work with have feelings and challenges. When you tell a personal story, the feelings generally come through and you will soon be viewed as a "real person" who is not so different from them. Your messages will become more highly valued and you will see more follow through. People in poverty may follow through because of the relationship at first, not necessarily because they see the program or assignment as valuable. Valuing education or training may come after the person experiences some achievement and success in the areas you are working on.

BUILDING IDENTIFICATION: SOME LEVEL 2 EXAMPLES

Example I: College Teacher/Student

During my first day of class at the University of Portland, I was overwhelmed by the big words and lengthy assignments. I walked into my third class of the day and the professor started his lecture by asking the students to "bear with him because he had just lost both of his parents and his 19 year marriage had ended." His hands were shaking when he talked. From this self-disclosure, I came to the realization that my professor was a real person and similar to me in some ways. He had feelings. All day, I had been so intimidated by the professors because they were all "Dr." somebody. Because of his level-two self-disclosure, I had the courage to approach him and ask him questions. Questions like, what does "Rhetoric" mean and what does "Dialectic" mean? He took time to answer and ended up being a significant mentor in my educational journey.

Example II: School Teacher/Student

Student: "I hate math. I am never going to be any good at it. I have tried, but math is not for me. No one in my family is good at math."

Teacher: "When I was 14, I thought I was dumb. I always got bad grades and teachers wrote all over my papers that I had done the assignment wrong. I felt just like you. I really believed that I would never be able to do math or any schoolwork. I was failing everything. Let me tell you what helped me. I had a teacher named Lewis who took the time to help me and show me that I was smart. All I needed was someone who knew how to do it to spend some time with me. Other kids had people who helped them. It took me going to talk with the teacher every day, but after a while, I got better and better. Lewis would tell me stories to help the math make sense. He was so happy when I finally started getting problems right he screamed and jumped in the air. I laughed my head off at him, and I kept coming to him for help. I got a B for the first time in my life in his class. I told Lewis I was failing my other classes and he helped me find nice people who really cared about me to help with reading and writing. Before that, I really hated coming to school, and I never thought I would be any good at school. Now, I am a teacher. I care about you, and I want to help you just like Lewis helped me."

Example III: Welfare Caseworker/Person on Welfare

Caseworker: "You need to apply for 30 jobs a week and keep a record of every application you turn in."

Person on welfare: "No one will hire me. I have no references, no education, and I have been in jail."

Caseworker: "I know how you feel. My brother Wayne had spent most of his life in prison and he dropped out of 8th grade. He and his family were on welfare and he did not think he was ever going to get off public assistance/welfare and get a decent job. I introduced him to my friend Eileen who helps people write resumes. She knew exactly how to make him look good. He had a lot of things going for him, but he was so worried about his prison record and having so little education he forgot to even think about what he was good at. Wayne learned there are a lot of employers who are willing to give someone a chance. He now works at the shipyards and he makes $27 an hour with health care benefits. You should see how happy he is to be able to provide a living for his family. He even made enough to take them to Disneyland this summer and his little girls are so excited. You have a lot of things you are good at and I want to see you do well. I bet my friend Eileen would help you too."

Level 3: Burke (1969) does not say that you have to go to Level 3 of self-disclosing your most private values and beliefs to build identification. Finding common ground with those you serve may be as simple as, "You like red, I like red." "I am a parent, you are a parent." And so on. Identification requires two-way interaction. With a deeper level of self-disclosure, you will also see how you are like the person you are working with, just as they see how they are like you. When this happens, people are much more able to take the risk of stepping outside of their comfort zones to try whatever it is that you are suggesting. When the teacher or social worker or helping professional knows something about the people they serve, they are much more likely to reach out and do what is truly needed to help the person move forward—including finding additional resources, opening doors of opportunity that were closed and connecting people to others who can provide help.

ACTIVITY 4: IDENTIFICATION

This group activity is useful to clarify the concept of identification and to invite people to reflect on the foundational blocks for building strong relationships. It can be done with any group of professionals working with people in poverty.

Script

"Please turn to the person next to you and:

- Introduce yourself to that person.

- Share three things the other person does not know about you and listen to three things you do not know about them.

- Make a short list of the ways you are alike."

Debrief

When we identify with people we are serving, we are better able to communicate and relate. We are in a better position to understand their behavior and responses and we are more likely to go out of our way to help.

The ways that you are alike provide the common ground for identification. I see how you are like me and you see how I am like you. Identification requires common ground. Common ground can only be built with self-disclosure. There are levels of self-disclosure:

1. Information Sharing

2. Using personal story or personal examples to explain

3. Gut level values

Most helping professionals stay at the information sharing level. This level does not build identification. Identification requires Level 2 self-disclosure: Using personal examples or personal stories to explain and clarify what you are trying to communicate or teach. This breaks down the us/them, or "professional as other" dynamic. If I see you as other, I may not trust or believe I can do what you are saying.

When I see you as a person who is like me and understands me, I can better understand your ideas, suggestions, and what you are asking me to do. I am more likely to step outside of my comfort zone and take risks—if someone like me has been successful at doing what I am being asked to do.

Relationship Development Theory

Relationships are social connections or attachments between two or more people that may be centered around something they have in common or be built on common ground. They vary in differing levels of intimacy and sharing. Knapp's relationship development theory (1984) offers powerful insights into how relationships develop and gives professionals working with people in poverty pointers on how to communicate, gain trust, and build strong connections with them.

Knapp's theory describes a process of relationship development that consist of five stages. According to Knapp, successful completion of each stage moves the relationship toward a more accepting, empathetic, understanding, and stronger relationship bond. In the final stages, a mutual feeling of trust is established and both sides become ready to work together to accomplish outcomes. Each side offers their strengths and they begin to agree and support ideas that may not fit into what they originally wanted or expected. They even begin to see that they are a team. For helping professionals working with people in poverty, pushing the relationship beyond "the initiation stage" helps them gain trust and become more effective in serving people from poverty. I have added information to Knapp's five stages to include applications for working more effectively with people in poverty. The five stages that Knapp identified for relationship building are:

Stage I—Initiation Stage: Refers to the first encounter two people have. This stage is very short, sometimes as short as two minutes. In this stage, the helping professional tends to be concerned with following office procedure, determining eligibility, or teaching a concept. The person in poverty tends to be concerned with getting basic needs met, being treated with respect, and feeling like they are accepted and that they belong. Both parties may use standard greetings and observe each other's appearance or mannerisms. Perceptions are often formed at this point and decisions are made. The professional may feel, "They just want a hand out" or "they just want to take the easy path," while the person living in crisis feels, "They just don't care about me." Most people living in poverty start to tell their situations, and then the professional, making assumptions based upon what they believe is going on in the lives of the person in crisis, does not really hear their stories.

In focus groups with people living in poverty (Beegle, 2000), the majority reported that they were interrupted within 18 seconds of explaining their situations to helping professionals. Fewer than two percent ever got opportunities to finish telling their needs. Almost three-quarters of the focus group participants reported that they left the interaction with the teacher, social worker, health care, or person working in the justice system saying, "I do not know what I am supposed to do next." People living in poverty emphasize the need for using familiar words and examples and giving them a visual image of what is going to happen.

Four recommendations from people who live in poverty for improving the interaction in the initiating stage are:

- Remember that they are people and be respectful
- Be as relaxed as possible and suspend judgments
- Be helpful and pleasant
- Show honest concern and smile

Stage II—Experimenting Stage: In the next stage, individuals start asking questions of each other in order to gain information about them and to determine what is possible. Both parties generally decide at this point if they will continue to make an effort. Many relationships progress no further than this point.

Professionals often decide that there are too many problems or make personal judgments (i.e. the individual is not being honest, won't follow through, etc.). People in poverty decide this is "a waste of time; I do not belong here; these people are not like me and/or do not understand me." People in poverty often are mandated by need or their situation to continue the relationship even if they feel it is not going to be helpful. Professionals are also often mandated to continue the relationship even though they feel it is not going to be helpful. Both people may have reached a dead end. At this stage, if the relationship has stagnated, it may be necessary to introduce a third party to help to move things forward and end the negative cycle.

Stage III—Intensifying Stage: If the relationship progresses, self-disclosure becomes more common in the intensifying stage. In this stage, people begin to discover their commonalities. The relationship becomes less formal, the participants begin to see each other as people, and statements are made about the level of commitment each has to the relationship and to following through.

In the intensifying stage of relationships between people who live in poverty and helping professionals, self-disclosure is often one-way with the person in poverty doing all of the self-disclosing. Power dynamics often interfere with relationship development (i.e. the teacher can take away recess, the social worker can suspend their welfare check). One-way self-disclosure is not sufficient to make a difference for the person in poverty.

People in poverty need the professional to reach out to them and self-disclose more than information. They need to find common ground with the professional and to be able to see them as a "real" person who cares; someone they can identify with and trust. Professionals can be successful in this stage by sharing personal stories, giving personal examples, and by telling how they learned the information being given so the person being helped can see the professional as a person similar to them in some ways. They need to see the professional as a person with challenges, feelings, problems, hopes, desires, traumas, etc.

To move to the next level of relationship development, suspend your judgments about people who are living in poverty and "see" them as individuals who are like you. Assume they are making the best decisions they can in the traumatic conditions of poverty in which they live. Focus on understanding even if you have limited time with those you serve.

Stage IV—Integrating stage: The individuals begin to work together to accomplish outcomes. Each offers their strengths and they begin to agree and support ideas that may not fit into what they expected. Others begin to see that they are a team working together. Each brings knowledge and insights for achieving goals and they are equally valued. The helping professional serves as a coach rather than the expert.

Stage V—Bonding: During the bonding stage, people begin to tell others about the relationship. The professional will talk about "someone they know" or their "mentee." The person in poverty may talk about a "teacher who cares," or "a friend" who is helping them. Few relationships between helping professionals and people in poverty reach this level, yet this is the level that makes the biggest difference.

Relationship theory provides a foundation for making a real difference. Having interactions where you or the person you serve is just sharing information will not build identification and is unlikely to promote the growth of those you serve. We have to move beyond our defined roles and find common ground to better communicate and understand. Whether it is a positive comment, a look that says I noticed you, or a bonded relationship, there is power in connecting. The connection can be two minutes or for many years. With every interaction, you have the opportunity to make a positive connection and to have the people living in poverty conditions walk away from you feeling like someone cares. That power is in your hands.

Social Capital Theory

Social capital theory can help break poverty barriers if it is used to connect people to resources and networks of support. Bourdieu and Wacquant (1992) defined social capital as the amount of resources an individual or group possesses by virtue of a network of relationships and connections. When Coleman (1988) introduced the theoretical model of social capital in an exploration of community effects on completion of high school, he defined social capital by referring to what it does, and argued that social capital exists in the relationships among people, and comes through changes that facilitate action. An example of social capital would be a person knowing someone who knows someone at a company where they wish to work. The prospective employee contacts the friend who contacts their friend resulting in an interview or a job. The saying "it's who you know" is more true today than ever before. It is how people get jobs, get into certain schools, and get doors opened for them.

Social capital is not tangible and therefore, difficult to grasp. Economic capital is wholly physical, embodied in material form. Human capital is less tangible, being embodied in the skills and abilities of an individual. Social capital refers to connections among individuals—the trust, mutual understanding, and shared values and behaviors that bind the members of human networks and communities and make cooperation possible. It refers to the institutions, relationships, and norms that shape the quality and quantity of a society's social interactions. It is the glue that holds them together.

Isolation perpetuates poverty. To break the isolation of poverty people need networks. They need to have at least as many people in their lives who have benefited from education and jobs as they have those who have not benefited. They need someone to help them see their situation from different perspectives, someone to use as a link into the worlds of education and work. People need someone they can call and use as a reference or who explain how to get the door to opportunity opened. The basic premise of social capital theory is that interaction enables people to build networks of support, to increase access, to commit themselves to each other, and to create opportunities for reaching potential. Building the social capital of people in poverty helps expose them to the norms, expectations and experiences of people who have succeeded in education or the labor market. It increases their abilities to fit in and understand the purpose of what they are learning or trying. Field trips and bringing professionals in to tell their life stories and how they came to be in the positions that they are all ways to increase social capital for people living in the isolation of poverty.

Building a person's social capital can be achieved by:

- Introducing them to your network. If you know their areas of interest, link them with someone who shares those interests.

- Exposing them to people who have benefited from education and jobs. Help them meet and get to know professionals. People need to see that those who are "making it" are not better than them. They are just people who have had different opportunities.

- Helping them build their own network of people who have experienced success and have easy access to society's services and resources. When you are in poverty, often everyone you know is also in poverty. Role plays of informational interviews, thank you cards, and follow up information on how the person is doing are all tools to help them build a network. People may need help with small details in making the connections like getting cards and stamps, acquiring appropriate clothing and transportation, and so on. It is vital to set them up for a successful exchange by role playing and providing what is necessary for follow through.

- Broadening their experiences and expectations. Field trips and bringing professionals in to tell their life stories and how they came to be in the positions that they are in are all ways to broaden possibilities.

An example of network building occurred when I was in the WIT Program. After helping us explore our interests, the participants were asked to do three informational interviews with people who were working in jobs they had expressed an interest in. I had identified journalism as an interest. The staff helped me in a very personal way to get phone numbers, to roll play what I would say, and to make it safe for me to step out of my comfort zone. My first call was to Pete Schulberg, a local news anchor. I was in awe that he actually answered the phone and even more in awe when he said I could come to the news station and talk with him about his work. He took me backstage and I got to see him read the news on the air.

Two months later, the WIT staff encouraged me to send him a postcard and update him on what I was doing. I did this again six months after meeting him. Shortly after that, he called me and took me out to lunch to discuss possibilities in journalism. We became friends and I had a person in my address book with a title and a phone that did not get disconnected.

Understanding and Communicating: Oral and Print Culture

The ways in which people give and receive information impacts their world view, and values, as well as their communication and learning styles. Understanding the preferred communication and learning styles of people in poverty increases our chances of successfully reaching out to them, establishing relationships, as well as learning about their strengths, assets, and resiliency characteristics. My personal experiences and research (Beegle, 2000) revealed that people living in poverty develop styles of communicating and learning that are very distinct from those of the middle class. Experience and research also showed me that a lack of understanding of these differences can explain why "helping" professionals have difficulty effectively serving people in poverty.

There are two distinct styles of communicating and learning—oral and print—that can be used to frame understanding and provide us with useful language to describe how to improve communication across class barriers. These two communication styles come from their respective cultural and contextual roots:

- Oral Culture (orality) is a natural state in which we are highly attuned to our senses (touch, smell, sight, sound, and taste) and devote a great deal of attention to sensory information. Orality emphasizes our interconnection with the environment and the people in it.

- Print Culture (literacy) is a learned way of relating to the world, where people learn to process and analyze (breaking things down according to parts) information collected through sight, sound, hearing, touch, and smell according to categories, classifications, and styles of reasoning developed by reading (Ong, 1982).

According to Walter J. Ong (1982), all people are born with a preference for oral communication and learn print communication styles if they grow up around adults who went to school and learned how to get information for living their lives through reading. Oral culture does not mean that a person cannot read; it means that people prefer to seek information for living their lives from other people or through verbal means, not print. For example, if someone is sick in a family, the print culture communicator would likely consult a medical text book or find an article about the illness. The more oral culture communicator would find a family member or someone who knew someone to ask about the illness.

From the context of poverty, I learned an oral culture style of interacting and processing information. When I learned about oral and print culture communication styles, for the first time in 1989, I finally had a language to describe my strengths and frustrations as I was being challenged to acquire print culture skills. However, research (Ong, 1982) affirms that both oral and print culture styles of communicating and learning have value. Each brings rich opportunities for human growth and connections. I also found that understanding the two styles of learning and communicating can break significant barriers for educating and working with people who live in poverty.

My mentor, Dr. Bob Fulford, told me I was the most oral culture person he had ever met. He said, "I want you to gain the skills of print culture, because that is what you need to be successful in the workplace and in education. However, I want you to maintain your skills of oral culture because many people in our society have lost the abilities to develop relationships, to see the big picture, and to be spontaneous." He always taught that in order to take care of ourselves and our planet, we needed to use the skills and strengths of each style as situationally appropriate.

The following chart shows the major characteristics of each communication and learning style.

Relationships: Are at the heart of everything and are first priority; they are more important than anything. When we need information, we ask those around us who we identify with.

Spontaneous: Strong desire for variety; great abilities to "go with the flow" or jump from subject to subject with ease. It is normal to interrupt and to have multiple conversations at once. Interrupting is seen as adding information. Likes to focus on lots of ideas at once.

Repetitive: Repetitive storytelling and repeating the same thing over and over are important for maintaining the knowledge. Telling the same stories over and over helps in understanding and with moving information from short-term memory to long-term memory.

Holistic: Focus on the "BIG picture," but not the details; tendency to take in everything that is going on around us. Highly in tune with environment. Often go to school or appointments not by a clock, but by what is on television or what is happening around us.

Emotional: Comfort with emotions. Shows emotion and feelings readily in most any situation and is open to self-disclosing private details. Sharing personal experiences and stories is our way of connecting with others.

Present oriented: Highly in tune with the here-and-now. Focus on what is going on around us right now.

Agonistic: Physical. Using the body is an important part of relating and communicating. In return, we display and expect a great deal of emotional and physical reactions. Touch and facial expressions are big part of learning and communication.

Linear: Organizes thought and actions by "first this, then this" thought process

Time: Is at the heart of everything and has high priority in daily activities. Time is crucial and we are rigid about it.

Analytic/abstract: Knowledge is outside of self. Demonstrates an ability to step back from a situation and separate and disconnect self from what is going on. It is important to think abstractly about situations and analyze them carefully, detail by detail before reacting. Do not show emotions or physical affection unless we know the person really well, and do not share personal stories. Facial expressions are limited. When information is needed, we look for a book on the subject.

Self-disciplined/focus: Strong ability to shut out sense data and focus on one idea at a time. Ability to separate and disconnect from the environment and personal emotions.

Ability to delay gratification: Strong understanding of relationships between parts; sort and categorize information.

Ability to strategize: Plan ahead, set goals, and focus on the future, ability to break things into parts, promotes ability to connect small efforts to end desires. Believe a plan is essential and the goal is to stay on task. Ability to organize efforts according to predetermined goals.

Future oriented: Focus on the future, and feel a strong sense of control over what it is going to be like. Ability to strategize, organize and delay gratification. Can execute plans for the future.

Strengths in Communication: Broadening Our Skills

Walter Ong (1982) strongly emphasizes that one style of communicating and learning is not better than the other. To be truly effective communicators, he asserted that people need to have the skills from both oral and print culture. Furthermore, he argued the ideal communication style is to be balanced; having the ability to maintain both the characteristics of oral culture (which keeps one connected and spontaneous) and the characteristics of print culture (which allows one to set goals, plan ahead, analyze, and stay focused). For example: if you need to be more relational, you can tap into your oral culture skills. If you need to be on time, you can tap into your print culture abilities.

Many people who are print culture communicators lose touch with their natural style of communicating and become so dominant in the print culture that they struggle to acquire some of the characteristics that oral culture people exhibit readily, such as the ability to develop relationships and to be in the moment. Likewise, people who stay steeped in oral culture struggle with print culture characteristics, such as breaking things into manageable steps or planning ahead.

There is a dominant belief in the United States that the oral culture style of communicating is inferior and requires less intelligence. However, there is evidence that oral culture has unique strengths. Many of the cultures that have been ecologically sustainable over hundreds or thousands of years are oral cultures. Many of the characteristics of these oral cultures (emphasis on relationships, respect of the limitation of the earth resources, closer connection to the earth and its cycles, less focus on material possessions, being in flow with relationships and time) are characteristics found in societies that live within the ability of the earth to replenish itself.

Print culture, while admirable in many ways, contains within it many of the characteristics that contribute to ecologically unsound ways of living; a focus on technological solutions; a "management" orientation towards nature; distancing self from others through abstract reasoning and reliance on print; a focus on material growth; a fast pace; and a relationship with time as a commodity. When one takes ecological sustainability as the ruler for judging culture, oral societies have much to be appreciated for.

Currently, the majority of our institutions are designed to honor, validate, and serve people with print culture skills. We send important information in flyers, handouts and letters. We write notes on students' papers instead of talking with them. We lose talent and potential by shutting out the gifts of oral culture and focusing only on print culture styles of learning and communicating. We have to find ways in our schools and organizations (which are largely print culture) to establish, value, and include some of the oral culture styles of communicating and learning. We must move to models that honor oral culture styles of communicating, while teaching the skills of print culture.

Effective communication is a necessary step toward eradicating the barriers to success for people to move out of poverty, and cannot be achieved without educating people on ways to broaden their repertoire and develop their less dominant style of learning and communicating. The following chart outlines a few basic steps toward teaching the skills of both print and oral culture.

Teach Skills of ORAL Culture	Teach Skills of PRINT Culture
• Pay attention to intuition and act on it. • Focus on how you feel and tell others how you feel about them. • Practice active listening to stay in the moment and to build better relationships. • Practice empathy to gain insights into how you are like others. • Respond immediately without thinking. • Stay focused on the moment. • Sing, dance, and be silly! • Pay attention to your environment. • Use gestures. Use lots of body language: express yourself with out talking. • Tell your feelings.	• Model reading as a primary source for gaining information they can use in their context. • Create lists. • Practice sorting and categorizing. • Practice outlining key points from the concepts being taught. • Break assignments into explicit baby steps—doable, manageable steps. • Show examples of completed work as models to follow. • Have people tell their life stories and then help them to write them down. • Give examples of how the "in the moment" behavior leads to future experiences.

Implications for Action:
Incorporating Oral Culture Skills into Your Service

The concepts of oral and print culture can be very powerful for those who work with people from poverty backgrounds. In particular, they can be used as lenses to look at the services professionals provide and examine the extent to which they meet the needs of the people they serve. By learning the characteristics of oral culture, helping professionals can acquire some of its communication skills and use them to reach out effectively to people in poverty. This does not mean that communication with people in poverty should solely be conducted along oral culture characteristics. People in poverty need to broaden their communication repertoire as well and need to learn print culture skills. Using the former can become a vehicle for helping people in poverty develop new skills, and broaden their prospects for success.

Incorporating oral culture communication skills into our interaction with people in poverty and the services we provide to them requires us to do the following:

1. FOCUS ON BUILDING RELATIONSHIPS

For people in poverty, having a trusting relationship with a professional is key for them to venture outside of their comfort zones and becomes a motivation to learn the new skills presented by the professional. Individuals from poverty, who are more oral, get their information by asking other people. It is easier to remember a story than abstract facts or out of context information. Relationships based on identification are critical for oral culture communicators. Print culture comes from reading; and getting your information from the written word. Having a good relationship with a professional entails access to reliable sources of information. As a professional, it is your responsibility to convey the needed information in a form that people in poverty can relate to. Make your examples contain lots of information about people—real people that you can tell stories about. For example, in a classroom, the teacher can personalize the information in just about every subject. Teachers can tell students who developed a certain theory or help students make personal connections to what they are trying to teach. Students from poverty connect to people, rather than abstract knowledge.

Developing a relationship that involves personal stories will allow those you work with to see why the tasks assigned are important and how achieving the requirements can mean something other than stress to them. By sharing from personal experiences and perspectives, teachers will help students understand (and internalize) the concepts being taught and why the subject matter is important.

Building these relationship also gives professionals an opportunity to listen empathetically to people's stories and to hear the reality of what their lives are like. Then, when explaining concepts, professionals can use concrete examples relating to the people's personal lives, not just unrelated examples from a middle class lifestyle, which will help them answer the question, "What does this have to do with me?" With the inclusion of examples from their own lives, concepts won't be so far removed from their world that they can't see their value.

Relationships are critical! Contrast that with the often-held beliefs that professionals "don't get personal" and "maintain their distance." There is a real disconnect inherent in this type of clinical professionalism. Individuals from generational poverty need strong and strategic relationships in order to overcome seemingly insurmountable barriers to their personal success.

2. IMPROVE COMMUNICATION THROUGH USING STORIES

Storytelling is an essential part of learning for those from oral cultures. The more storytelling you can do around concepts, the more effective your communication will be. It can be really powerful. If you can describe how something happened to somebody by relating it to personal experiences, they're going to learn more than if you describe it as an abstract concept. Personalize the information and they'll get it. If it's abstract, it's hard for them to grab on to.

3. ALLOW TIME AND FLEXIBILITY FOR SPONTANEITY

Individuals from poverty tend to exhibit the characteristics of spontaneity. They tend to be very comfortable jumping from subject to subject, which is the nature of oral communication. On the other hand, with print, people are more linear. The word linear (l-i-n-e-a-r) means nothing unless those letters come in that particular order. Reading trains our brains to think in terms of first-this-then-that, and we organize our lives accordingly. For example, think about the "first-this-then-that" teacher working with the "spontaneous" student. There's such a contrast and clash in communication styles. A student will talk about many things at once, and then the teacher will be unable to follow and will say, "Okay, wait! Now, tell me what happened first."

Oral culture teaches skills for taking in a lot of information at once. The print culture communicator learns to process one idea at a time. This helps explain the struggle for understanding by a print culture communicator when multiple people talk at once or there is a lot going on. Print culture which comes from reading trains the brain to shut out sense data. You can not understand what you read if you are paying attention to other sensory inputs. Oral culture trains the brain to process as much information.

4. USE REPETITION

Repetition is important for oral culture people because they store information in their short-term memory. It made sense to be repetitive when print was not a common form of communication, because the knowledge would be lost if it weren't repeated. Knowledge that is not used in one's daily life is discarded. That's why you can tell oral culture people something and then a little later they may say, "You didn't say that!" If they didn't see the relevance of the information right away, they had already discarded it. Print culture people put knowledge outside of themselves. They write it down, and then, come back to it if they need it. Print culture people have access to a long history of knowledge. Printing and orality are just two distinct/different ways of storing, receiving, and communicating information.

According to research, people remember:

• 10 percent of what they read

- 20 percent of what they hear

- 30 percent of what is visually presented

- 50 percent of what they see and listen to

- 70 percent of what they say

- 90 percent of what they verbally repeat and apply

Thus, the most powerful way to present information to people is to have them say it and do it. Verbally repeating and applying the information sends it to long term memory. When information enters the brain, it goes into the prefrontal cortex and decides what to keep and what to discard. Unless the information is meaningful, it is discarded. For people living in poverty what is meaningful must be connected to their life experiences and current context. It is important to connect to as many memories as possible for retention and understanding.

5. UNDERSTAND THEIR IMMEDIACY AND HELP THEM BUILD SUPPORTS TO PLAN FOR THE FUTURE

The immediacy of oral culture and the crisis of poverty doesn't always allow for a focus on the future or to strategically plan ahead; so individuals from poverty may tend to focus on what they're going to do today or what they're going to do tomorrow rather than on long-term goals.

Since the words said are gone shortly after they are spoken, oral culture people learn to be in the present in order to get the knowledge. Educational barriers are compounded by poverty in that immediate needs take precedence: Where are we going to sleep tonight or what are we going to eat tonight?

Print knowledge comes from outside of the individual, training the brain to think abstractly and analytically. Self-discipline comes from the ability to shut out all senses and not pay attention to everything that's going on, focusing on that one idea. The ability to delay gratification comes from seeing how all of the parts fit into the whole, and knowing what's going to happen. For oral culture people who live in poverty, the feeling is if it doesn't happen right now, it's not going to happen.

Print culture people are future-oriented. Often they find that they "aren't really there" in the moment. They are abstractly thinking about what they are going to do (for example, what are they going to do when they get home, what are they going to have for dinner, etc.). They tend to not commit themselves to the moment, remaining somewhat aloof and detached in their relationships.

Linear people tend to focus on time. Print culture is about breaking things down into tiny little parts. It means nothing for a print-culture person to say, in the middle of a conversation, "Gotta go or I'll be late," which may sound rude. That abruptness won't happen with an oral culture person. They will continue to talk until there's closure even though it means they're going to be late for their next appointment.

But what do middle class social norms say about people who are late? The behavior is value judged as disorganized and rude based on what a middle class, print culture person would do.

The spontaneity of people from oral culture makes them very skilled at handling crisis situations and last-minute tasks. You can throw your oral culture individuals a last-minute task and they go with the flow. Going with the flow and staying with whatever comes up is a strong part of oral culture. But they will have a more difficult time with a plan. They are not as accustomed to stepping back and planning things long term. For example, what happens to long-term assignments? Teachers often assign something with a due date, possibly reminding students the evening before it is due. The oral culture students will have completely forgotten about the assignment and will try to complete it that night. The nature of oral culture combined with the immediacy of poverty-related needs take priority over remembering an appointment or assignment. Constant repetitive reminders are needed if you want oral culture communicators to remember something.

6. BREAK THINGS INTO "BITE SIZE" PIECES

For oral-culture individuals, professionals will need to break things down into little parts. Don't just give them a large assignment and ask them to complete the entire thing. Remember, they are likely experiencing crisis and may be overwhelmed with the amount of information required and have difficulties breaking tasks down into manageable, doable pieces. Before they leave, model how to plan for the completion of the activity by setting up benchmark steps along the way. Most of the things they are asked to do by helping professionals are usually outside of their experience and comfort zones. They don't have a frame of reference for being successful in middle-class endeavors, and they need a lot of encouragement and support in order to experience small successes. Every day, reinforcement is essential for them to begin to feel like and maintain the attitude of "Okay, I can do this."

7. ALLOW FOR CONNECTING AND RELATING WITH EMOTIONS

Oral-culture people are more likely to laugh, cry, and show emotion. They look for non-verbal responses signaling that they're okay, and that there's a possibility for them to be successful. Constructive criticism is a middle-class concept. Oral-culture people will take it personally. When I speak, it's my tone, gestures, and inflections that help give you an indication of who I am. This is where the "everything-is-personal" statement comes in. If you say, "We're not going to talk about that right now, Donna," you're not rejecting the subject matter, you're rejecting me. I am whatever subject matter I'm talking about. Oral-culture people have not had experience in distancing themselves from the subject matter—they are the subject matter. Thus they are more likely to respond physically and emotionally to their environment (pat you on the shoulder, slap you on the back, etc.).

Print culture teaches people to distance themselves from their emotions. Most of the time individuals with an oral orientation don't see the helping professional's non-verbal communication because they are not expressing a lot of emotion when they speak. They are often viewed as cold, uncaring, and non-human. Conversely, professionals tend to ignore emotional displays as outbursts and ask people from oral culture to be calm. Rather, what they need is to understand that for people in oral culture, most communication is non-verbal, forcing them to use and to pay attention to everything around them in order to get the meaning, knowledge, and information that they need to get through their day.

Helping professionals also need to accept that by freely expressing their emotions, oral culture people are making genuine attempts to communicate and reach out.

FIVE POWERFUL COMMUNICATION STRATEGIES

People from poverty backgrounds shared the following communication strategies that made a difference in their lives:

1. Telling stories—use vivid examples to allow people to feel the impact of what they are doing.

2. Modeling appropriate behavior in supportive ways.

3. Developing relationships based on identification while sharing information.

4. Using simple, familiar words and examples that people can relate to.

5. Giving information verbally, often, repeatedly and with good eye contact.

(Beegle, 2003)

In conclusion, professionals need to first learn about the differences between print and oral culture, and then help oral-culture individuals to understand themselves and their communication style. People need to have a language to describe how people communicate and why they communicate the way they do; understanding that it's all about how we send and receive information. To help oral culture people learn new skills we need to:

• Make them feel confident. Self-confidence affects the ability to remember. Help them to not focus on and internalize mistakes, but to focus on what they have done well.

• Spread-out repetition is most effective. Have them make a list. Set it aside. An hour later, look at it again. An hour after that, look at it again. This helps transfer the information to long-term memory.

- Share information in multiple ways. Hearing it, writing it, seeing it, and creating models of it all help with recalling information.

- Have people imagine an image of what they want to remember. If it is a date or a name, give an image to associate it with. For example, "My name is Donna Beegle, like the dog, but with two ees." This is a mnemonic device that can make a difference.

What's most important is to continue to reflect and dialog about how you can apply this information in your environment and in your work. Find ways to make space for individuals from oral culture to have some of their knowledge, experiences, and communication styles valued. Help them maintain their oral skills while gaining the skills of print culture; which will help them be successful in education and in the world of work.

Mentoring: Pulling It All Together, Being the Bridge

"We ourselves feel that what we are doing is just a drop in the ocean. But the ocean would be less because of that missing drop."—Mother Teresa

Traditional Mentoring

Traditionally, mentoring referred to a relationship between an older, more experienced guide (the mentor) with a younger, less experienced partner (the protégé/mentee). The relationship helped guide the youth through their growth and development with a mix of support and challenge. In this sense, it was a developmental relationship where the younger person was introduced to the world of the older, more experienced adult (Hamilton, 1991; Freedman, 1995). Traditional mentoring included the characteristics of providing expertise, advice, and examples to enhance educational opportunities, advance careers, and help people build their professional networks.

Donna, 15, with "mentee" Lynda, 5

Two types of relationships are defined in the literature on traditional mentoring: formal and informal. Informal relationships develop on their own between two individuals. Many people have "natural mentors" as they move along the different stages of their life journeys. These people might be aunts or uncles, grandparents, neighbors, pastors, or family friends. A mentor can also be a trusted friend, university professor, counselor, coach or teacher. These natural mentoring relationships most often occur in middle-class environments.

However, the isolation of poverty results in limited opportunities for connections with people who have succeeded in education or employment. Mentors with the experience or personal connections to nurture mentees on their journey through an education system or assist them in connecting to good jobs are hard to come by for those struggling in the crisis of poverty. Formal mentoring programs—meaning assigned relationships often associated with organizational programs—have developed to fill this gap. These social service programs work in a variety of ways and are developed and/or funded by a range of supporters (such as faith communities, government programs, community-based programs with or without any formal affiliations).

Some schools have formal mentoring programs for new students or students who are having difficulties. These youth mentoring programs match caring, concerned adults with students who may be at risk. The adult is usually unrelated to the student and works as a volunteer through a community, school, or church-based social service program. Many studies have provided evidence that youth mentoring has many positive outcomes for everyone involved (Herrera, 1999). Both formal and informal mentoring programs share the common goal of strengthening the chances of success and advancement through a mentoring relationship. However, for people living in poverty, these traditional mentoring relationships may not be long enough or strong enough to build the trust needed for successfully moving out of poverty.

CURRENT RESEARCH

In Levine and Nidiffer's book, *Beating the Odds: How the Poor Get to College,* they reported that all of their research participants from poverty who made it to college had mentors. They also reported a strong correlation between the length of the relationship, the number of mentors, and the highest academic degree attained. The participants in their study who made it to elite private universities had mentors prior to the sixth grade, and those mentors handed them off to other mentors as appropriate for supporting their educational journey. The participants who made it to community colleges had been connected to mentors later in life. Levine and Nidiffer's research found that anyone could be a mentor, but there are specific characteristics of mentoring that have the most impact on children and families in poverty. The findings from my research (Beegle, 2000) are consistent with Levine and Nidiffer's work, with my research identifying additional characteristics that are described below.

One of the primary findings from my research was that people from generational poverty who were successful in the educational system all had someone who went above and beyond to show them they were special; someone who understood and did not judge them for their poverty circumstances; someone who believed there was a way out of poverty for them; someone who talked with them when there were barriers; and someone who introduced them to others who supported their educational journey and helped them to build confidence. This someone (or someones) ensured access to resources they could use to meet their basic needs and overcome roadblocks to completing their education. Another key finding was that the mentor relationship often extended beyond the student to the student's family. Mentors made positive connections for brothers, sisters, mothers, cousins, and even in some cases grandparents. My study participants reported feeling relief from worry when they knew someone was helping not only them, but also the people they loved.

Mentor relationships that break poverty barriers are built on trust. Trust is essential for stepping outside of what is normal and trying something new. The theory of social capital presumes that the more we trust the more we connect, and the more they connect with us the more they trust and reach out to us (Coleman, 1988). Putnam (1995) suggested that communication that facilitates access to information and resources that helps the individual to achieve their priorities is a large component of building trust. The mentor's role is not only to help with academics, but to build social capital—meaning connecting students to networks of people and supports that can help them on their journey.

Mentoring relationships that are strongly grounded in trust facilitate opportunities to identify with others and, in many cases, share their own experiences of poverty. Mentors must be someone the mentee can identify with. Participants in my study (Beegle, 2000) reported that, once they identified with their mentors (saw how they were like their mentors and felt they were accepted for who they were), they felt safe and began to trust their mentors. Having a successful mentor who did not judge them helped raise their self-esteem and resulted in stronger relationships. Then they were able to self disclose and share their poverty-related experiences, that helped them to begin to externalize some of their shame and pain from poverty. As they externalized the poverty, mentees reported an understanding that it was not their fault and allowed them to begin examining some of poverty's systemic root causes.

> *"For the longest time I actually believed that we were to blame for the way we lived. I thought that we had done something wrong and that's why we did not have food. As I met more and more people I learned it was much more than behavior or choices. Some people in this society are privileged; they have not done anything special to earn their class standing. Just like people who are poor have not done anything to earn their poverty. It is about who has the opportunity and generally who you know."—Carol*

Additionally, through their mentors and connections, participants were able to hear life stories about the mentors and how they came to be who they are. These realizations helped participants know that their mentors were not better people—that they just had more opportunities and resources. Some reported surprise at learning a mentor had gone to the same school for more than a year. They assumed people were in their positions because they were smarter or better people. Hearing the stories help participants to see their mentors as just people who had different opportunities and experiences.

Self-disclosure is a also two-way street that often transmits powerful benefits to the mentor. Most middle-class people are often amazed when they finally realize the conditions of poverty and discover the resourcefulness necessary for survival. Having the opportunity to hear the stories of those who grew up in poverty conditions is a powerful and transformative experience, often generating additional support, connections, and asset building. These stronger relationships created an environment in which helping professionals were more likely to show respect to their mentees and were better able to provide appropriate assistance.

Participants reported "modeling" and learning middle class norms from their mentors. These relationships expanded their repertoire of communication skills and helped them acquire "print culture" skills and behavior that helped them integrate more smoothly into their college community. Mentors gave them permission to ask questions that most people seemed to already know. My research (Beegle, 2000) showed that mentors, and in some cases the mentors' connections, were pivotal to linking participants to information and support that facilitated their success in moving out of poverty. For example, participants reported that their mentors helped them to learn to navigate the middle-class systems (such as financial aid, study habits, and connections to resources like computers or extra academic help) that in turn increased their access to resources. These resources, in some cases, were also used to assist participants' families with their living conditions, thereby reducing the stress and worry of poverty conditions by participants and allowing them to focus on their studies.

Mentor Characteristics

Anyone can be a mentor, but for improving opportunities for people in poverty, there are specific characteristics associated with success. The following mentor characteristics were identified in Levine and Nidiffer's (1996) research and my own research (Beegle, 2000). These characteristics are not presented as an add-on to the jobs of those working with people in poverty, rather, they present an invitation to professionals to redefine their approaches to service and build it around the principles of inclusivity and mentorship. By following these simple guidelines, helping professionals are more likely to be successful in achieving their organizational goals of moving people out of poverty. Mentors effective in breaking poverty barriers have the following common characteristics.

Successful mentors:

1. Believe in the individual. Sadly, too many people in poverty say they cannot think of one person who is educated or earning a decent living that believes in them. We must surround people in poverty with at least as many people who have succeeded in education and careers as the number of those in their lives who are struggling with poverty

2. Believe there is a way out of poverty. Often, helping professionals see the multiple poverty barriers that people are facing and they feel it is too much for them to overcome. If you believe that people cannot grow and learn because of their poverty, it will be difficult to help them.

3. Open your personal network to these individuals and teach them how to build their own networks of support. If you know someone who has some expertise or support that can help those you serve, make the connection.

4. Are educated about poverty and have a multicultural awareness:

   • Understand structural causes of poverty

   • Are aware of the history of poverty in the United States

   • Know poverty-related facts about your community

5. Suspend judgment; because they know that if they are judging, they cannot connect, and, if they cannot connect, they cannot help.

How to be a Mentor

Anyone can mentor, and effective mentoring can be at different levels. Below are five strategies for effective mentoring.

1. Meet people where they are and find common ground, self-disclose, and build identification (Burke, 1969). "I am like you—you are like me."

2. Connect to resources to help with basic needs—especially housing, food, transportation, education, and training (Maslow, 1943).

   • Example of resource connections: Organizations can host "flea market" settings with food and resource information about careers, school, housing, and other relevant information to those you serve. Providing usable information builds trust (Putnam, 1995).

   • Use community partnerships to avoid being overwhelmed and burning out.

3. Identify strengths and abilities, and provide opportunities for success (Strengths Perspective, Saleeby, 1997).

4. Identify areas for growth and build individual success plans (Beegle 2000).

   • Break down goals into doable steps with success and rewards built in along the journey—considering their context (building resiliency and assets).

- For each activity on the success plan ask: Is the activity out of their reach or out of their comfort zone? Do they have the materials and supports necessary to complete it? (i.e. If the activity is to cut out pictures from magazines, do they have any magazines? If you ask them to go somewhere, do they have gas or transportation?)

5. Help them build a network of successful people that have benefited from education. Introduce and expose them to new experiences. Identify areas of skills/interests and connect them with professionals who are doing these things. For example, if someone is interested in art, introduce them to an artist. (Social capital theory, Coleman, 1988)

An example of a highly successful mentoring program is Friends of the Children that practices the long-term commitment to children in poverty and has had terrific success in increasing graduation rates. Friends of the Children started in Portland, Oregon, and now operates in eight states. The program pays "friends" (mentors) a teacher's salary to mentor kids from first grade through 12th. The "friends" (mentors) make a long-term commitment to the children and, as much as possible, stay in contact even if the child moves.

Levels of Mentoring

From focus groups with students, educators, and tutors (May 2006), we have found that there are four levels of mentoring—each requiring varying degrees of time commitment and resource development and producing different types of relationships between the mentor and mentee.

Impacting comments: Does not require a long-term commitment or even a dedicated relationship between two people. Here, a trusted adult can provide a truthful passing comment that leads a young person to take a certain path.

> Example: One day a male high school student was greeted warmly by one of his trusted teachers. The teacher said, "You remind me of my brother who is a lawyer. I bet you would make a great lawyer yourself." Without saying anything else or conversing further about this statement, the two parted. The teen kept this comment in his memory for years, finally graduating from law school. The teacher never knew the impact the one statement had on this particular student.

One-way mentoring relationships: Many young people tell stories of the one adult that had a tremendous impact on their life. They talk about how the individual consistently treated them in a specific (nurturing) way and all the little things that changed their lives. Often, in these types of relationships, the adult never knows the impact they have had on the young person until many years after their time together has ended. Sometimes the adults often complain to others that they have done so much for the young person and see no changes in their actions or appreciation for what has been done. These relationships are often time specific (during a school year, a one-year commitment to a volunteer tutoring contract, an after-school/extra-curricular activity, or team sport).

> Example: In high school, one female teenager who was living in the crisis of poverty was taking a journalism course from one of the language arts teachers. The teacher recognized a lot of potential in the student and went out of her way to praise the efforts the student did and prompt her to work outside her comfort zone. Because the teacher knew the family situation of the student, she assisted the student with getting extra resources that were out of the reach of her family and helped connect her to people in the community that could serve as role models and form a network of support for her. The student seemed to take the extra assistance for granted and never discussed it with the teacher or thanked her for her assistance. After graduating from college with a degree in journalism, the student went back to the high school to look up the language arts teacher. She told her how much her assistance was appreciated and how it helped her decide on a path for her life.

Two-way mentoring relationships: These relationships can be time specific or long term. The main difference between the one-way and the two way is that the adult in this relationship knows about the impact they are having on the young person and continuously gets feedback from the person they are mentoring. The mentor continues in the relationship through good times and bad, and is committed to being available for the young person even if there is a break in the relationship for a time.

> Example: A school counselor was working with a young girl in an elementary school. She helped the young girl through some difficult family times and connected her with appropriate peers within the school. Although they remained close throughout elementary school, the two lost touch after the girl went to middle school. When the counselor took a position at a high school in the area, she discovered that the teen was also at that school and began assisting her through some of her educational choices. After graduation, the counselor continued her relationship with the young woman assisting her with her secondary education choices, relationship issues, and employment options. In addition, the young woman worked as an office assistant for the adult—helping her with all the tasks that she could not accomplish on her own.

Relay mentoring relationships: This relationship starts between two people with the mentor assisting the protégée in whatever way is most appropriate. When the protégée has outgrown the specific assistance the mentor can provide or when they identify another need or area of interest, the first mentor introduces the protégée to another mentor how can better meet their needs. Sometimes the first mentor stays connected with the protégée during their time with the new mentor. Other times, the first mentor hands the protégée off and may reconnect again once the second mentor has completed their time with the protégée, thus moving in and out of the protégée's life and connecting when needed. Other times, the relationship ends when the first mentor is no longer needed.

Example: My life story contains many examples of they type of mentoring relationship. I was mentored by the women in the WIT Program who introduced me to the staff at MHCC who could assist me with my GED and 2-year degree. The staff at MHCC helped me to connect with the staff at the University of Portland. There, I met Dr. Bob Fulford, who became a mentor to me and worked with me through many issues, then introduced me to others who could assist me on my pathway to my doctorate.

Another example is the relationship I had with 17-year-old Mindy. I met Mindy when she knocked on my door and asked to use my phone. She was dressed in dark black clothing and had so much make up on I could not see her face. Within a few minutes, I learned that Mindy had spent most of her life in poverty struggling with hunger and homelessness and watching her family suffer. Our initial mentoring was around helping her find housing and advocating for her in the school system. I connected her to a vice principal who had grown up much like Mindy, and she began mentoring her through her senior year. I also introduced her to a school counselor who helped her sort out her feelings about her life and build her self-confidence.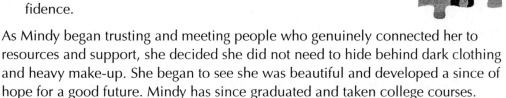

As Mindy began trusting and meeting people who genuinely connected her to resources and support, she decided she did not need to hide behind dark clothing and heavy make-up. She began to see she was beautiful and developed a since of hope for a good future. Mindy has since graduated and taken college courses.

In sum, mentor programs were designed as a service that was separated from the work of the four groups of helping professionals who primarily work with people  living in poverty. If we are to make a difference for people living in poverty, those who work with or care about people in poverty must incorporate the role of mentor into their efforts to help. While that may sound impossible to the social worker, teacher, person from the justice system, or health care providers, and others who have little time, the mentoring necessary to break poverty barriers is different than the traditional mentoring models and can be done in multiple ways. Making a strong connection with people in poverty may require more up-front time, but if we have a job that requires us to help people move out of poverty, the research is clear. This connection, this mentoring, even if it is time limited, is essential.

ACTIVITY 5: MENTORING IN PRACTICE

The following pages contain three family stories. They represent a cross-section of people living in poverty. There are "traditional nuclear families," single parent families, and families with extended family living nearby. There are issues with unemployment/underemployment, mental health, incarceration, alcoholism, and drugs. Middle-class people often struggle with these issues as well, but have resources to get the professional help they need. The family members described below are real. I have changed names to protect their privacy, but the stories are real. The families struggle with being successful in school, finding the right job, locating appropriate housing, and having their basic needs met.

Please choose one family story to review. This will be the family situation that you work with. We will be presenting you with ways to serve these families better within the capacity of your organization. We have outlined some questions below to help you think about these families and to formulate ways in which to help them move out of the situations they are in.

What strengths does this family have? What are some of their protective factors? What are their assets?

What more do you need to know in order for you to build a relationship with this person/family? How will you go about building a relationship with this person? How do you feel about this person/family? How do your feelings determine the level of commitment to helping them?

How would you be their mentor/guide? What common ground do you have with them? Do you have a connection to resources that they might need?

Could you help this individual/family build their social capital? Who do you know that they should be connected with?

Is it possible for this family to move forward? Why or why not?

If you knew this family's situation what would you do to help them? In your role within your organization, how can you help this individual/family?

CORY, ROSY AND FAMILY

Cory is the youngest of six children and the only boy. Growing up, his family lived in poverty and was often homeless. His father told him that he did not need an education because he was supposed to take over the family sign-painting business. However, the "family business" had no regular customers and required door-to-door cold calls. Cory attended school sporadically. His father enrolled him only because they had no food at home and knew the kids could get a free lunch at school. Teachers once visited the travel trailer where they lived in an attempt to discuss Cory's low academic skills, but his father felt threatened and shut the door on them. Cory never received an education past 12 years old. As an adult, he reads at about a fourth grade level, is not artistic and never followed his dad's plan to be a sign-painter.

Cory (age 31) now lives with his girlfriend, Rosy (age 29), and their three young daughters. For a year, the family lived in a rented storage shed. Without an education or network, Cory struggles to provide for his family but works extremely hard. He gets up early in the morning to attend car auctions where he buys vehicles for under $50. He creatively solves problems everyday through the challenge of getting the cars home through illegal towing. Most of the cars do not have license plates or have not passed DEQ and he risks getting traffic tickets. He works long hours to fix the cars and then sells them to make a small profit. Through this hard work, he has become a self-taught mechanic. However, he battles with the law because he cannot afford to become a licensed auto-dealer. He illegally uses the names of friends and relatives to purchase the vehicles and occasionally gets caught by police, ticketed, and fined. He cannot get a job at a mechanic shop because he does not have a mechanic's license and cannot read and write well enough to fill out the necessary customer paperwork.

Because of the stress and struggle to provide for their family, both Cory and Rosy turned to using and dealing drugs for about five years. They have been off the drugs for several years, but their poor appearances hinder their job search: their teeth are rotten, they cannot afford decent clothes, they speak nonstandard English, and they have difficulty filling out job applications.

Their oldest daughter, Shelly, spent most of her life feeding and caring for her two younger siblings while her parents were into drugs. She is knowledgeable about all her families' struggles. She energetically answers the home phone and talks to callers about the cars they have for sell. She is the "go-between" for her parents and other adult relatives—working with them to help solve her families' problems, such as discussing how much money her parents are behind in rent or asking to borrow money for food and promising that her parents will pay it back when they sell a car.

At school, Shelly is talkative, expressive and assertive. However, she gets in trouble frequently for pushing and shoving other children and not minding the classroom rules. She bosses classmates and talks back to the teachers. She has been sent home several times for her behavior. When she gets sent home, Rosy loses her temper, hits her across her shoulders, and yells at her for not doing better at school. She then makes Shelly watch her younger siblings while she tries to solve another daily crisis.

TRACY, DON AND FAMILY

Tracy grew up homeless living in cars and campers with her family in isolated parts of the California and Nevada desert. To escape an unstable and lonely life she married, at 18 years old, the first man she ever dated, a military man named Don. Tracy's parents suspected that Don was mentally unstable but were unable to persuade Tracy to leave him. She was merely happy that someone wanted and loved her. The couple spent the first ten years of their married lives living a working class, military lifestyle in a tiny rural area of Missouri with limited socializing.

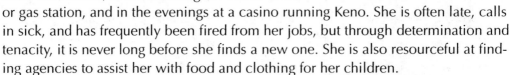

Eight years ago, Don got out of the military and the family moved to Nevada. He has not held a job since because of his worsening mental illness. He talks about absurd things, such as aliens or the government watching him through the wires in the streets. He stays at home and is the primary caretaker of the four kids.

Tracy works three minimum wage jobs to support the family. Throughout the night she works at an elder care center, in the mornings at a mini-mart or gas station, and in the evenings at a casino running Keno. She is often late, calls in sick, and has frequently been fired from her jobs, but through determination and tenacity, it is never long before she finds a new one. She is also resourceful at finding agencies to assist her with food and clothing for her children.

From the day she was born, Hannah, the youngest of Tracy and Don's children, has been cared for primarily by her mentally ill father while her mother works several jobs. She just entered pre-school this year. Two months into the school year, the teacher called and informed Tracy that Hannah is "mentally retarded" because she is lacking in verbal and social skills, wets her pants throughout the day, and speaks very few sentences or words. She mostly sits quietly in her seat and looks scared. Tracy initially took in the information without much response, but later she cried for hours. Out of embarrassment and fear that Hannah would be taken away because of child abuse, she did not inform the teachers that her husband is mentally ill and has been the only adult caring for Hannah since she was born.

With high aspirations to provide a better life for her kids, Tracy talks about becoming a substitute teacher in K-12 schools. The job would provide enough money so that she could work only one job and be home for her kids in the evenings. In the state of Nevada, she would qualify to substitute teach if she passed three tests. However, juggling several minimum wage jobs does not leave her any time to study for the tests. In addition, she never has enough extra money set aside to pay the test fees.

MOLLY AND KYLE

Molly grew up with her four sisters, one brother, father, and mother. Molly's mother could not read or write. Her dad believed that she and her sisters did not need an education because, like their mother, they would get married and their husbands would take care of them. Her parents were both extremely unaware of the importance of school and did not require her to attend. When the family stayed in a town for a few weeks to a few months, her dad would enroll them in school—mostly because he did not have any money to feed the kids. They also had no money to provide her with any activities or hobbies that would help her reach her potential. By 13 years old, she stopped attending school.

The family moved from campground to campground—never having stable housing or friends. Molly says she felt very lonely growing up, so she married young to start a family of her own and find the love and companionship she had been missing. She gave birth to her first child, Kyle, at 17. Her goal was to be a stay-at-home mom, but the relationship dissolved when Kyle was two years old. For the next five years, Molly spent all her time fighting a custody battle. She went to the library and checked out books on the law and read extensively. She knocked on lawyers' doors and begged for help. Her tenacity led one lawyer to take her on as a pro-bono case. However, in the end, with no home stability and no formal education or job history, she lost full custody of Kyle. But because of her extensive research, she gained an extensive law vocabulary and thought about returning to school to become a lawyer. But she had no knowledge of college processes and no one to show her how to become a lawyer.

Because of the ingrained belief that she should marry and be supported by a husband and no one to show her how to become a lawyer, Molly returned to the isolation of poverty. Through loneliness and a desire to have a family, she focused her efforts on finding a husband. Soon she met and married a man. A year later she gave birth to her second son. A few years later, poverty destroyed that relationship. Within a year, she met another young man, who was also living in poverty, and married again. Together, she thought, they could make a decent life. A year later, she gave birth to a baby girl, but within six months the stress of trying to earn a living destroyed that relationship.

From the time he was three years old, Kyle, now 13, has been going back and forth between his mother and father's homes. Because Molly never emotionally healed from the dissolution of her marriage and bitter custody battle, she frequently talked negatively about his father and the father's wife when Kyle came for his weekend visits. Recently, Kyle's step-mom discovered that he had sexually molested his younger half-sister and sent him to live with Molly. Overnight, Kyle went from living a middle-class life at his dads' to struggling in poverty with his mom. At a younger age, Kyle had been an energetic, athletic boy. Now he is withdrawn and quiet, and sits for hours playing computer video games. At school, he gets in trouble for inappropriate social behavior and is behind in academic skills. His main interest is in art. He spends a lot of time drawing detailed, colorful pictures; however, they are of violence, darkness, death, and vicious animals. He is also likes to tell imaginative, unrealistic stories. His teachers say that he is lacking in maturity and has a negative attitude.

Molly now has all three children living with her and none of their fathers have education or training to earn a living wage. Therefore there is no child support. She is often homeless with her children—living in her car, cheap motels, or relatives' living rooms. The rest of her siblings and parents live in poverty, and she does not have anywhere to turn. She feels lonely, lost and depressed and longs for a husband to take care of her.

Understanding the Context and Lived Conditions

In Section 1 (A Foundation for Understanding Poverty), you were given generic information about the state of people in poverty in the United States. Then in Section 2 (Serving People in Poverty) you were given theories and strategies for working with those you serve. But one of the key points I would like to stress is that to be able to effectively serve the people with whom you work, you first have to get to know them as individuals. Once you have learned about the history of poverty and the systemic barriers that keep people poor, it is crucial to learn about those you serve and the situations that confront them on a daily basis. Knowing a person's context and what they care about helps the professional to effectively motivate them and build on their strengths and assets.

Please use the following two activities as steps towards understanding a person's context and living conditions in order to become more informed and sensitive to the needs of those you serve. This information will also provide you with language and examples related to the lives of those in poverty.

ACTIVITY 6: SCAVENGER HUNT

Activity 6 is an immersion scavenger hunt that will help you build a better under-standing of the needs of those in poverty in your own community and the resources available to them. Your goal for this activity is to gain a deep understanding of what your city/local area looks and feels like for those you serve.

This activity asks you to visit some of the places within your community and learn firsthand about the services available and some of the peripheral costs of living in poverty. Many of the pieces of information can be found online or by placing a few phone calls to the correct individuals. Not all actions will require that you go to the agencies providing these services to complete this activity. However, for the most impact, personally visit one or two of these agencies/organizations to get a feel for the environment, to see/hear how the individuals are treated, and to analyze the messages they receive (both intentionally and unintentionally). Even though you can find some of this information via an internet search or phone call, there is NO substitute for "experiencing" what those living in poverty experience on a regular basis and immersing yourself in the context which those you serve experience on a daily basis. The experiences in the scavenger hunt will also provide you with relevant examples to use for building connections and increasing your trust with people you serve.

The Scavenger Hunt has been divided into nine groups with scenarios to personal-ize the hunt to a family situation that may be affecting those you serve. The indi-vidual group "hunts" seek information on income sources, housing options, food, transportation, health care, money, miscellaneous household goods, and educa-tional options. The hunt, as outlined, provides generic examples of areas to explore. If you have time, provide specific information about places to visit and locations of organizations. For this activity, divide the participants into small groups. Pro-vide phone books, maps, and access to computers in order to help the participants fulfill the requirements of the activity. Set a time period of 2 to 4 hours, depending on the geographic proximity to the locations and the time available for this activ-ity. You will also need to set aside time to debrief the activity once participants return. When participants return, seat them in their traveling groups (if more than one group went to the same place, combine those groups) and ask them to identify some key findings from their "hunt." Encourage personal reactions and challenge any stereotypes that come up in the discussion. Ask participants to discuss in their groups how their experience relates to helping people who live in poverty and have them share this with the larger group.

Group 1: Income

Until a few years ago, things had been going rather well for you and your wife. You had been given a couple of promotions within your company and worked your way up from the bottom levels to a more middle management position without the benefit of a college education—through your hard work, determination, and the knowledge and skills learned on the job. But shortly after giving birth to your youngest son, you wife passed away from complications during surgery. Within three months of her death, you are involved in a head-on car accident with an uninsured motorist that leaves your right leg shattered. You are out of work for 6 months, work part-time for three months, then return to your job full time. Within five months of returning to work, your company loses a major contract and lays you off. You realize because of your work situation in the past year, you will not be eligible for the maximum benefits you would have received before the accident. Also, because of your limited education, your chances of being hired for a job similar to the one you just lost will be extremely difficult. Additionally, you are still walking on crutches and will continue this way for several more months—leaving you feeling less capable of presenting your best self to a prospective employer.

Action	Answer
Review web site: www.dol.gov/esa/minwage/America.htm. Find out the **minimum wage** for your state.	
Review the web site for your state **employment office.** Find out how to qualify and get benefits. Use your Internet connection to look up the benefits someone would get by making $40,000 for several years, then compare that to what they would receive with only $15,000 in the last year.	
Visit a **welfare office** in your area. Pick up an application for food stamps and cash benefits. Find out how much in monthly benefits a single parent with two children receives on welfare and disability when they have no assets and are on the verge of homelessness. How much would they get if they had one more child? Sit in the office for 20 minutes. Notice how people are treated and listen to how they are talked to. Pay attention to the environment. After the 20-minute wait, go to a "receptionist" and ask how long the average wait is to speak to a caseworker to get assistance.	

Group 2: Housing

You are a parent of three children. You have been in a battering relationship for several years. You have put up with the abuse for the sake of the children, but your partner has just recently begun turning his/her aggressions towards the children. You have always stayed home to parent the children so you have no job and no money of your own (to rent a place to stay or provide the necessities for your children). You have been estranged from family and friends so you have no one to turn to and nowhere to live.

Action	Answer
Review web site: www.huduser.org/datasets/fmr/ fmrs/select_geography.opb. Find the **average price** (fair market rent) for a two-bedroom apartment in your city.	
Call a **domestic violence shelter** in your city. Find out about their services and how someone qualifies to receive services. Find out how long a person needs to wait to find a bed for herself and her children. Find out the average stay in a shelter. Find out what kind of assistance they receive from the organization to help them get back on their feet. Find out if there are services for men who have been in abusive relationships.	
Visit a local **motel** and find out what the daily and weekly rates are. Ask how much notice must be given for you to move out. Find out the rules and restrictions (Can you cook in the unit? How many people allowed? Etc.). Imagine living here with your children. What are your concerns?	
Visit a local **Housing Authority office.** Find out how long the waiting list is for Section 8 housing. Ask how to get housing if you are poor and elderly or disabled. Ask if there is housing available to single males. Pick up any materials that can be used for further information.	

Group 3: Housing

You are a married couple with two children of your own. You are also raising your two nephews who lost their parents in a car accident. Together you earn $15.00 an hour. One of you has been hurt on the job and must now survive on disability. Your credit is horrible. You have a criminal record and multiple evictions.

Action	Answer
Review web site: www.huduser.org/datasets/fmr/fmrs/ select_geography.opb. Find the **average price** (fair market rent) for a two-bedroom apartment in your city.	
Visit an **apartment complex** in a poorer section of your city. Find out the price for a two-bedroom apartment. Is there an application fee? How many people are allowed to live there? What is included in the rent? How much is the deposit? Do they require a credit or criminal history check?	
Visit an **apartment complex** in an affluent section of your city. Find out the price for a two-bedroom apartment. Is there an application fee? How many people are allowed to live there? What is included in the rent? How much is the deposit? Do they require a credit or criminal history check?	
Compare the two properties. What did the property look like? Feel like? How were you treated?	
Find out the **average utility bill** for a two bedroom apartment in your area: (ask the apartment managers) • Electricity • Gas • Water/Sewer • Phone • Cable Call the utility company or use the internet to find out how many people get their water and electricity shut off in your city per month.	

Group 4: Food

You and your three children (ages 3 months, 1 year, and 4 years) live in a low-income housing complex in a run-down neighborhood in your town. You have no car and have to rely on public transportation to get around town.

Action	Answer
Review web site: www.fns.usda.gov/fsp/applicant_recipients/fs_res_ben_elig.htm. Find out how much in food stamps a family of four can get for one month. Browse the web or do the math to find out the federal allotment per person/per meal.	
Take a few minutes and figure out what you would serve your family (of four) on this for a month.	
Review web and find out about the Woman/Infant/Children (WIC) program. Find out what benefits you qualify for and how to get signed up.	
Call a **food bank** in your city. Ask: What are the contents of an emergency food box? What is required to receive a food box? How often is the service available?	
Visit a grocery store and a convenience store/mini market in a low-income neighborhood in your city. Write down the price of several of the items, including a loaf of bread, gallon of milk, package of toilet paper, and one "luxury" item (candy bar, 6-pack of beer/soda, etc.).	
Think about what it would be like to buy groceries for a family of four and then take these home via bus with three small children.	
Visit a grocery store in an affluent neighborhood in your city. Compare the environments of the two stores. Compare the meat and produce departments. Talk about what the environments of the two stores say about the way the store feels about it regular clientele. What messages does this send to the people who shop there.	

Group 5: Transportation

Until recently, you have been driving around town in your new Hyundai. One afternoon, you are driving home from work. You reach down to get your ringing cell phone and cause a head-on motor vehicle accident. You come out with a broken ankle, but have severely injured the other driver. You had let your insurance lapse in order to pay other bills, so your license gets suspended. You must now rely on public transportation.

Action	Answer
If you have public transportation in your town, drive to a central location, park and take the train or bus to downtown a local homeless shelter. (If no public transportation, drive to the shelter.) Find out what services are available and what you need to do to qualify. Get information on what is available if you were a senior citizen and needed housing tonight. Pick up any materials that can be used for further information.	
If you have public transportation, go to their ticket office/information center or visit their website. Find out how to take a bus to a local DMV from the ticket office. Find out how to get to your place of work from your home. Bring several schedules and information back to share with the group.	
Go to the local DMV. Find out how much it costs to reinstate your driver's license after it has been suspended. How much does it cost to get tags for your car?	
If you get a chance to ride on public transportation, notice who sits by whom? Think about what it would be like to have this as your regular mode of transportation. Imagine having to make several trips to several different offices to get your needs met...all the while towing several small children along!	
What is the price of gas in your city? Using 20 MPG as an average for most cars, how many miles will you get on a 20-gallon tank? How much does it cost per gallon?	
Call an insurance agent to find out how much more your car insurance would cost if you had gone without insurance for a while. Find out about an SR 22 filing: What is it for? How long is it in effect? How much does it cost to insure a car with this?	

Group 6: Health Care

You are 17 years old and have a one-year old child. Until recently, your mother has been clean and sober. She had been trying to straighten out her life and help you take care of your child and finish school. But recently, she was introduced to meth at a party and has given herself over to the drugs again. So, you have had to drop out of school to get a job to care for yourself, your child, and your mom. You work two part-time jobs at a fast food restaurant and a clothing store...both only giving you 20 hours a week so they don't have to pay for benefits.

Action	Answer
Call the local County Health Department and tell them that you need an emergency dental appointment. Inform them you have been in pain for two weeks but have no insurance or money. Find out how much it will cost, and how long you have to wait to get in.	
Call and find out about the health plan that is available to those in poverty in your area. What are the requirements to get coverage? How long is the waiting list for medical and/or dental care once you have insurance?	
Visit (or call) a local drug rehab center. Ask them what resources are available for a meth addict. Find out the waiting time for services and what is available to the people while they are awaiting services. What is available to someone in poverty without insurance who needs rehabilitation or mental health services? Pick up any materials that can be used for further information.	
Visit a local teen parent program. Ask what they have to offer to a teen mom who is a high school drop out on the verge of being homeless. Pick up any materials that can be used for further information.	
Visit a local health clinic. Find out how long the wait is to see a physician. Sit in the waiting area for a bit (as long as time allows) and notice how people are treated and listen to how they are talked to. Pay attention to the environment. What do signs say in the waiting area? Are clients greeted immediately and given assistance in navigating the system or are they left to figure things out on their own. Is there enough information and translators for those who do not speak English?	

Group 7: Money

Your elderly mother lives in a town over 300 miles from your home. One afternoon you get the call that she has suffered a severe heart attack and they don't know if she will make it. You must go to her and be with the family during this time. But you have no cash to buy gas…or a bus ticket…or plane ticket. And no one to borrow it from. What are you going to do?

Action	Answer
Visit a car title loan company. Find out what documentation you need to get a cash advance and how much it will cost if you pay the loan back in six months.	
Visit a commercial check-cashing service/payday loan organization. Find out what documentation you need to take out a payday loan. What is the limit on the loan? Find out the terms and conditions for repaying the loan. Find out how much it costs to cash a personal check and a government check.	
Visit a pawn shop. Find out: How much they will give you for one of your personal jewelry items. How much it will cost to get it back.	
Take a few minutes to look through the stuff in the store and find out how much they are selling items for. Find something that looks of similar value to what you were going to pawn and compare their selling price to what they are willing to give you for it.	
Describe how it felt to visit one of these places? What did it feel like to have to use your possessions in order to get the cash necessary to do what was needed for your family? How can you use this information to better serve the families you work with?	

Group 8: Household

You are a middle-aged woman who has a teenage daughter. For 20 years, you and your husband have lived an upper-middle class life in New Orleans, Louisiana. He is a lawyer and you have been a stay-at-home housewife—managing the home, taking care of your daughter, and helping him get ahead in his business. You have also been very active in the Arts and have been instrumental in several charity organizations. About 2 years ago, he asked for a divorce. He was very generous in the divorce—paying off the house you lived in so that you and your daughter could stay there and leaving all the personal belongings. He provides child support on a regular basis, but no spousal support because of the housing arrangement.

When Hurricane Katrina hit, your home was completely destroyed and you lost all your belongings. While you were married, your husband had always handled such things as insurance policies. After the flood, you call him to find out who you need to contact to get you back into your home (and restore your previous lifestyle). He said he had paid for the house, but the insurance was up to you. You are left without anything. You are shipped off to Oregon to try and rebuild your life.

Action	Answer
Visit a local clothing closet. Find out: What is required to obtain clothing? How much clothing is given per person? How often is service available? Ask if they can help pay rent or utilities—if so how much and how long does it take.	
Look at the available items. Talk about how you would feel, as a teen in high school, to be wearing these items around school. What could this do to a person's self esteem?	
Visit a rent-to-own, no credit needed, furniture store and a regular department store. Compare the price of a television set and a home appliance (washer/dryer, fridge, etc.). What are the monthly rental fees for each? How much will you have paid for each item when you finally own it? What is the monthly payment if you had good enough credit to charge it at the department store?	

Group 9: Education

You are now 18 years old. You have grown up in a urban city—bouncing back and forth between your parents' "home" and various foster placements. When you were about 16 years old, your mother died from complications caused by AIDS. You ran away from the foster home they placed you in and lived on the streets for several months. You held down a job in the evenings as a dish washer in a restaurant and went to school during the day, but the schedule soon got to be too much for you. You finally dropped out of school. You love reading and it has kept you going through several of the more unpleasant times during your life. It has also helped you be able to keep up in school when you were going. You know you would like an education to help you create a better life for yourself. You consider going back to school for your GED with the hopes of getting a college education.

Action	Answer
Visit a local community college (or look up this information on their web site or call): Ask about their GED Program. What do you need to qualify for entry? How long does it take? How much does it cost? What additional benefits and resources do they help the students find? Find out if they have a transitions program or a program for displaced workers. Find out who is eligible for this program. Find out what they do and how they help individuals in the community. Continue reviewing their web site to see if there are other programs available for students from poverty backgrounds.	
Visit a local high school: Find out what resources they have available to poor/homeless students and their families. Find out if they have any special outreach programs for students who have dropped out of school. Find out what they need to qualify for special educational programs within the school.	
Visit a local college/university (or review their website or call): Visit the financial aide office. See what students have to do to qualify for financial aide. Ask how much money a person can get if they are a homeless, emancipated youth. Review the paperwork and try to determine what obstacle some students may have in navigating this system.	

ACTIVITY 7: FACING POVERTY

Activity 7, Facing Poverty: Laboring Against Its Challenges, is designed to help you learn about the resourcefulness required to survive in poverty in the Unites States. Once you take the test, you will have a better understanding of how people manage to survive without the resources that people from middle class have at their fingertips. People in poverty are incredibly resourceful and often have to "make do" with whatever they have. This activity is aimed at raising your awareness of some daily struggles people living in poverty may face. Many of you will answer, "I don't know," to most of the questions. This only means that your life experiences are far removed from the lived realities of people in poverty. This is not a test to see how much you know, but rather an invitation to research these questions as a way to better know the everyday living conditions of those with whom you work. You can also reflect on what strengths and assets are necessary for survival and begin building on those strengths as ways out of poverty.

The following are skills that could be needed in the context of poverty. Please answer the questions to the best of your ability.

Question	Answer
How would you get by for three weeks while waiting for your first paycheck?	
Explain how you would get food stamps or welfare assistance.	
Where can you cash a check without any identification? How much will it cost?	
Where can you get a loan on your car title? How much will it cost?	
From which dumpsters can you get returnable cans and bottles without being caught?	
How can you get tons of newspaper and cardboard to sell at recycle centers? Where can you sell these items? How much will you get?	
What would it take for you to move out of your house with a 72-hour notice?	
Explain what to do if you are being evicted and have no money to move.	
Explain what you would do to survive without garbage service, utilities, or a telephone.	
Describe how to survive winter nights without heat.	
Cite where you would go for help if your utilities were being shut off.	
How would you show "proof" that you live in a neighborhood that you really do not live in order to get better services?	
Explain how to go for days without food.	
Which stores will let you get food and pay for it later?	
How do you keep food cold without a refrigerator?	
How could you prepare a meal without owning a stove?	
How can you use a butcher knife as a potato peeler?	
How could you get your car fixed without any money for parts or a mechanic to help?	
How would you feel if you had to drive with no license or insurance?	

Question	Answer
Explain how to fix a toothache with super glue.	
Describe how to get free medicine samples at an emergency room if you are sick.	
How would you deal with waiting for hours for health or social services in a room filled with people who are hungry, homeless, sick, and desperate?	
Which church or agencies give free clothes and shoes?	
Which church or agencies have free clothes that are unstained and free of holes?	
Describe how you can wash clothes without money, laundry soap, or a machine.	
Explain how to use torn-up clothing for toilet paper, sanitary napkins, etc.?	
How can you find out what jail your relative has been taken to and the court dates?	
What are the rules for visiting people in prison?	
Where would you find a bail bondsman to get a relative out of jail?	
Explain how to give off an aura of violence to avoid trouble.	
Describe how to smoothly change the subject to avoid answering humiliating questions.	
Explain how would you feel when every day there is a crisis: e.g. you, a family member, or someone else you love has been arrested, evicted, had the heat shut off, is sick, has been kicked out of school, is out of food or has had their car towed?	
Would you know how to laugh if you were hungry, being evicted and had nowhere to go?	
How would you entertain a group of friends with no food, drinks, money, or transportation?	

Honoring The Voices
From Generational Poverty

My doctoral work (Beegle, 2000) involved interviewing people around the state of Oregon who grew up in at least three generations of poverty and who now have a bachelor's degree. We extensively discussed what it felt like to come from poverty, what kinds of things worked for them, and what recommendations they would have for people working with individuals from poverty.

Sharing my experience of growing up in generational poverty, along with the voices of these research participants, can contribute to your understanding of what is necessary for increasing the opportunities for success for those from poverty backgrounds. People in poverty have much to tell us about the struggles and challenges they face on a daily basis, and we often ignore their voices, assuming that we will be better experts in figuring out how we could help them. Alleviating the impact of living in poverty and making a difference in the lives of those in poverty need to be part of a comprehensive, collective effort that takes into account the perspective, world view, and recommendations of people who are experiencing and have experienced poverty.

The voices of people in poverty need to be present for key decision-making processes as we move into action. We not only need these voices to understand their world view, but we also must ask them what solutions will work for them. We must listen, honoring what they say, and asking them what they would like for their lives. Listening to these voices forces us—as a society—to confront the inadequate ways in which we organizationally, intellectually, and professionally deal with social class differences and face up to the shortcomings of our systems in serving all people honorably and equitably. Inviting people from poverty to share their views is a compelling step toward empowering them to define their hopes and dreams. While doing that, we need to focus on their strengths and help them build capacity and expand their networks.

Including these voices can also initiate a dialogue on the harsh realities of social class for people who have the misfortune to be born into poverty in the United States. These discussions must include all sectors (educational, judicial, health, and social service) and aim at unraveling the root structural causes of poverty and inequity that contribute to perpetuating the cycle of generational poverty. Only with this dialogue can we begin to understand what is motivating and truly develop responsive organizations.

Recommendations

One of the major goals of my work has been to open a space in which the voices of individuals who have grown up in generational poverty could be heard. I conclude this section with suggestions from participants in my research for improving educational opportunities for students from generational poverty backgrounds. Their responses were insightful and reflective, and I've presented their thoughts in their words. We can increase the opportunities for success for people from poverty if we first honor their voices—learning to hear and understand how they would like us to help and to work with them to end poverty.

RECOMMENDATIONS TO PEOPLE IN POVERTY FOR GETTING EDUCATED OR TRAINED

1. Get started even if it's a small step. You don't have to be perfect the first try. You are there to learn. Do it one day at a time, one paper at a time.

2   Believe in yourself. Don't accept being told you can't. Ask, "Why, how, and what can I do to make this work?"

3. Develop a relationship with a mentor who tells you that you are capable and who will help you through the system.

4. Tap into your survival instincts and learn the system. Make a point of understanding the rules and policies and make them work for you.

5. Take any opportunity to learn and acquire new skills. Talk with your trainers, teachers, and professors; ask questions.

6. Meet people and let them know your situation. Don't think others are perfect. They have just had different opportunities. Listen to other people's stories. It helps you gain a different perspective on your experiences. Then you can look at yourself and the world in context.

7. Don't be afraid to ask for help; everyone does.

8. Realize that it is okay to break out from your old familiar world and broaden your horizons.

9. When you make it to college, make sure you connect with at least one professor. Force yourself to remember you have a right to learn. If a professor isn't helping you, there may be better ones for you. You are the consumer.

10. Talk to people who work in the field you desire to work in.

11. Look for people who have traveled along this road and made it out of poverty.

Communication Across Barriers

RECOMMENDATIONS TO TEACHERS/TRAINERS

1. Acknowledge growth whenever you see it, regardless of where your students are starting. Affirm assets and gains in ways that provide hope and build confidence. When you see them struggling with assignments or performing below the expected level, make sure to ask yourself if a poverty condition/issue may be the root cause of this struggle. Find out what it is and examine how it may hold them back. Look at where they come from and continue to be generous in praising their successes.

2. Reflect on your own biases. Recognize poverty as a diversity issue. It is a way of life with many attributes that may not be obvious. Pay attention to class issues in the same way you would for obvious differences, like race or gender.

3. Make the classroom comfortable. Start on the first day by stating everything clearly even if the information seems obvious or you think that everyone already knows it. Repeat often.

4. Be approachable. Don't just assume students will come to you for help, go to them. Open the door (break the ice) for students who don't trust or aren't used to talking to a teacher. Convince them that you really want to help them succeed and your door is open for any questions no matter what. Walk there with them. Show them how to find you. Call them by their first name and make a point to get to know them.

5. Diversify your curriculum and make education relevant not only to the lives of middle-class students, but students of all class backgrounds. Include experiences of people who are poor and incorporate concrete, oral culture learning styles in your teaching strategies.

6. Remember that if your students aren't learning your subject matter, it's your responsibility to do something about it. Examine ideas about who can learn and what the role of the educator is in the learning process. Find out who in your class is struggling or doesn't seem to be fully participating. Talk to them; invite them in. Ask students what is difficult for them (both privately and in class)

7. Recognize that not everyone is the same. Don't assume that everyone shares middle class experiences.

8. Help students become aware of resources such as tutoring, social services, scholarships, mentor programs, and housing. Make it a class assignment to find resources and report back. Have the right attitude and show a willingness to help.

9. Share your stories of how you came to be educated and have others in the class share theirs. Self-disclose through personal stories in order to help students see that they are like you and you are like them.

10. Join a support group for teachers who also work with students from diverse backgrounds.

RECOMMENDATIONS TO ADMINISTRATORS/LEADERS

1. Use policies to serve people, not to punish and exclude them. Rethink rules and broaden or revise them to include poverty realities.

2. Make sure there are scholarships or funds to support individuals in need.

3. Understand that without meaningful help, people from poverty will not get a fair and genuine opportunity for success.

4. Mandate poverty-sensitivity training for all your staff.

5. Support and reward your staff for exploring the subject of poverty.

6. Create an organizational climate that recognizes the injustices and challenges of poverty.

7. Provide more services on site that are specific to the needs of individuals from poverty.

8. Conduct organization-wide discussions to become more educated about the realities of poverty in the United States.

9. Organize your institution's activities/services to allow time to build personal connections with the people in poverty that you are trying to serve.

10. Be a hands-on leader—make a personal effort to know and understand people from poverty. Learn their language.

RECOMMENDATIONS TO ALL ADVOCATES/SOCIAL SERVICE PROVIDERS

1. Don't ignore poverty realities. They won't go away. Address the real life situations people are in. Connect with people. Build relationships and trust. This demands more time, effort, and energy.

2. Encourage them to further their education, give them examples of how they can achieve and succeed, show them how they can have more than a low-wage job. Know about financial aid process and be able to simplify and help students from poverty to see possibilities.

3. Develop programs that meet people's basic needs so they can focus on education and other possibilities. Fund extracurricular activities focused on ensuring that students can read and understand math and science.

4. Work to change negative perceptions of people who are in poverty. Build relationships and understanding with them instead of judging. Operate on the assumption that people in poverty are doing the best they can in their situations. Understand each case and do not label people. Get rid of stereotypes.

5. Change some rules. Make the rules less based on middle class values and priorities. Understand what the world of poverty is like. Study cases and change the criteria to fit the realities.

6. Be more aggressive with outreach for access to health care, housing, and basic needs for those experiencing poverty

7. Understand that people who are poor may have fears or negative attitudes about education and other social service organizations. Work to give them a new positive frame of reference.

8. Help them with life skills and with "intercultural communication" in order to understand middle class culture and what is perceived as normal behavior in that culture. Uncover the secret codes. With middle-class expectations as the dominant adopted norms in our society, they need to know what people from middle-class cultures eat, and how they talk, dress, act, and speak in middle-class environments in order to overcome the challenges these differences present to them. Set up mentor programs where it's safe to ask questions about these things as well as health care, basic needs and education.

9. Be an advocate and make connections for people who do not have networks of support. Show them conceivable possibilities and help them see how they can achieve them.

CHAPTER 3

LAYING THE FOUNDATIONS FOR INSTITUTIONAL AND SYSTEMIC CHANGE

CURIOUS

I find myself more late with every crisis

more angry with every injustice

more greedy with every deprivation

more rude with every judgment

more disorganized with every eviction

more negative with every untreated illness

more unstable with every insecurity

I find myself more civil with every bite

more respectful with every kindness

more hopeful with every chance

more grateful with every opportunity

more ready to learn when I am safe

more motivated when there is hope

more happy when I am valued

I find myself like the 37 million people in poverty

responding in very human ways to my environment

—Donna M. Beegle

Poverty...The Unspoken Diversity Issue

"Poverty is not made by God, poverty is made by man and his unwillingness to share." —Mother Teresa

Poverty needs to be placed at the center of our struggle as a society toward achieving equity and social justice. We need to address the problem of poverty with the same intent and determination we are investing in our struggle to eradicate racism, sexism, and all biases, and to promote tolerance for diversity and respect for our individual and cultural differences. The social-class framework reveals the structural inequities (such as low incomes, inadequate housing, experiences of hunger, and limited access to resources) that shape the lives of people in poverty. The framework also points at the policies and organizational structures that prevent people from poverty from having genuine opportunities for social-class mobility and perpetuate the cycles of poverty.

Poverty is rooted in economic problems and social pathologies too deep to be overcome by improving schools or any other single "helping" agency alone. Given the tragic situation of those in poverty, a narrow approach may be too weak an intervention for improving the lives of most people now living in poverty. Our society lacks a comprehensive system of educational and social public policy that would be favorable to realizing the inherent potential of all humans. People born into poverty in the United States will likely remain poor throughout their lives (Levine & Nidiffer, 1996). The gap between their basic needs and resources ensure that without increased incomes, those born into poverty are unlikely to lead independent lives and fulfill their basic human needs, let alone achieve financial prosperity (Gil, 1992).

Breaking down social-class barriers would require systematically exposing the causes of existing individual, social, and economic problems in the structure and fabric of society, rather than disguising their causes, as is done now, by blaming individuals and groups for their problems and deprived circumstances (Gil, 1992).

The underlying political and economical reasons behind poverty must be addressed to end poverty and to promote an environment of equity and justice. As a society we have made significant efforts to accommodate the needs of middle-class families. The same effort is needed to accommodate the needs of families struggling

---

with poverty. We need to transform our existing social policies by having measures to "rescue" those in poverty rather than help them barely survive and simply manage their conditions. The current paradigm that emphasizes the "deficiencies" and "failures" of people from poverty and confronts the faults of the current system that allows poverty to continue must be challenged in order for us to move from a "coping" approach to an approach that moves people out of poverty conditions.

As a culture, we have an unrealistic faith in individualism and the power one has to change and improve their condition. As a result, we tend to "blame" those who "fail" to make it, because, if we don't, we'll be forced to acknowledge the limitations of an individual's efforts and to question our beliefs and familiar ways of operating within our organizations. Yet, that is exactly what is necessary. Making a difference requires that helping professionals take a comprehensive look at our systems and question their effectiveness to serve people in the crisis of poverty. We need to recognize the barriers that block change and perpetuate the conditions that cause poverty. The structural basis for our failure to end poverty is political, economic, and cultural. It does not have to be this way! We know how to help people move out of poverty. We know what works! There are success stories all around us. A comprehensive examination of our current systems is long overdue. As many have suggested, we need to reconsider our collective views about the proper and improper roles of government in ameliorating the problem of poverty; our beliefs about the ways in which our economy is supposed to work; our peculiar American ethos of individualism; and our almost absurd belief that schooling alone is the cure for whatever ails society (Anyon, 2005; Beegle, 2000; Berliner, 2005). Certainly there are changes schools can make to increase educational success for students living in poverty. However, without housing, food, and other basic needs, these changes may not last long enough or be strong enough to help someone move out of poverty. No Child Left Behind policies should also apply to health, housing, food, and safety. Then we would truly see no child left behind.

There is ample evidence that spending more money helping those in poverty does make a difference. Research has confirmed that improving income reduces poverty (Beegle, 2000; Berliner, 2005). The National Center for Children in Poverty (Koball and Douglas-Hall, 2004) found that the policies supporting education for low-income parents and children offer them the potential for lasting economic security. Furthermore, they wrote, "Temporary Assistance for Needy Families (TANF) provides policy makers with the opportunity to support education for low-income parents. It is critical that low-income parents, particularly those transitioning off TANF, have the opportunity to pursue higher education. The federal government should not restrict the educational programs that count toward TANF work requirements."

We also need to increase our ability as a society to collaborate and coordinate the services of our various institutions. This cannot happen without making a collective moral commitment to creating a society with no poverty—a society in which everyone gets the help and support they need, and no one is ever left alone, fighting for survival. Social programs such as disability and welfare should truly be a safety net, providing support appropriate for today's cost of living. As a society, we need to push for accessible health care, quality education, judicial systems focused on rehabilitation, the prevention of crime, and a livable wage that ensures a life of dignity for all.

Most of our well-intentioned attempts at helping people in poverty are either too fragmented, offer insufficient and limited support, or are built on an inaccurate understanding of the lived conditions and needs of those in poverty. While efforts to change the structural conditions that cause poverty should be in place and ongoing, there is much that can be done within our institutions to ameliorate the situation of people in poverty and increase the likelihood for them to succeed.

There are seven areas for improvement:

1. Fostering partnerships and collaboration among helping professionals to secure additional income and resources to overcome inadequate income, housing and knowledge barriers.

2. Developing an organizational climate that is non-judgmental and sensitive to social class and poverty issues. Acknowledging and confronting the issues of discrimination toward people in poverty are the first steps for most institutions. Developing a supportive climate includes the following:

   • Raising awareness and understanding through mandatory poverty sensitivity trainings

   • Creating a public dialogue on poverty and social class that includes the voices of people in poverty

   • Developing a no tolerance policy toward poverty discrimination that is similar to an institutional policy on racial and gender discrimination.

3. Adding the role of mentor to the job description of helping professionals.

4. Facilitating connections to informal and formal mentoring.

5. Interpreting current policies in a way favorable to people in poverty, and exhausting all currently available possibilities for support.

6. Going beyond caring and coping models—working differently, providing more connections to resources, and building relationships with people in poverty. If you cannot help, find out who can.

7. Being an activist to increase awareness for others to see how it benefits everyone to help people in poverty overcome the obstacles they face.

Organizational Culture and Change—Theoretical Foundations

My approach to change is built around the strengths perspective (Saleeby, 1997) and several organizational theories of change, most prominently Peter Senge's (1990) vision of a learning organization, Edgar Schein's view of organizational culture and leadership (1992), Cooperrider's (2000) appreciative inquiry, Tanner Pascale and Sternin's (2000) positive deviance, and Yvonna Lincoln and Egon Guba (1989) fourth generation evaluation.

The strengths perspective (Saleebey, 1997) underlies the proposed action plan for organizational change. Among others it serves as a distinctive lens for examining the assumptions that guide our practice. The strength perspective provides a way of thinking about human behavior, events and interactions. It is based on recognizing and focusing on the strengths that a person or a group of people bring to a context and develop change plans that build on those strengths. It proposes that every person should be treated as if her or his potential is unknown. The core ideas of the strengths perspective theory are empowerment, inclusion, and hope. If your organization's focus is to look for possibilities in the people you serve, you will develop policies and practices to support finding them. Current organizational policies and practices toward people in poverty often focus on problems, control, and deficits. People in my research reported rarely, if ever, participating in an organization where their strengths were acknowledged. The changes they were asked to make made little sense in their context of poverty.

In his seminal book, *The Fifth Discipline: The Art and Practice of the Learning Organization,* Senge (1992) identifies five important areas for positive organizational change: systems thinking, personal mastery, mental models, building shared vision, and team learning. Senge's incorporation of mental models with the organizational change process is especially important since the work with issues of poverty has to do with changing the deeply ingrained assumptions and images that influence how we understand the world and how we take action. Senge's understanding of the systems nature of change, along with his understanding of how deeply imbedded our habitual responses to the world are, make his theory central to creating organizations that work to help people move out of poverty. Considering the context, the big picture that people in poverty face empowers people in the organization and those who are being served to move forward.

Schein (1992) clarifies the concept of organizational culture and its relationship to leadership and change. His work explains how organizational values and beliefs form and solidify to become the lens through which people see their world and choose their actions. Schein postulates that without a good understanding of our organizational culture, there is no hope for a sustainable change. His theory provides us with a tool to become aware of our deeply ingrained organizational beliefs, analyze them, and develop processes and approaches to change them. What does your organizational culture say and believe about the causes of poverty and the people who live in it? In this book, Schein's theory is used as a framework for recommendations and strategies to transform organizations in a way that stops them from perpetuating poverty, and allows them to become more responsive and effective in meeting the needs of people in poverty.

Cooperrider's (2000) appreciative inquiry and Tanner Pascale and Sternin's (2000) positive deviance are two theories that focus on the positive potential of organizations and of people and the creation of new solutions where old ways of understanding no longer meet our needs. For decades, we keep doing what has not worked in our service to people in poverty. We focus on fixing people in poverty rarely considering how to create organizations that support movement out of poverty. Appreciative Inquiry has inquiry as a fundamental principle, believing that human systems grow in the direction in which they persistently ask questions. For example, "If you focus on problems, you will find more." *Positive Deviance* (2000) suggests that we find the positive exceptions to the rules and explore these options—bringing these "positive deviants" into the mainstream—what works and how do we do more of that! Altogether, these theories provide the foundation for approaches to change found within these materials.

The Communication Across Barriers© approach to organizational change is also based on the conception of "evaluation" outlined in Yvonna Lincoln and Egon Guba's *Fourth Generation Evaluation* (1989). Fourth generation evaluation emphasizes the role of the "stakeholders" in determining the criteria and goals for program evaluation. With its emphasis on how people create meaning and construct their reality, it keeps us focused on the contextual factors that shape these constructions, and provides us with a powerful approach to evaluation as it shapes and sustains organizational change efforts. The Fourth Generation theory forces a focus on reaching the outcome of ending poverty for those we serve.

Individuals and organizations serving people in poverty must actively apply change theory. This requires examining individual attitudes, beliefs, and values as well as organizational culture and norms. What we have been doing to eradicate poverty has not worked.

Toward Building Responsive Organizations

Success flows not from any single approach or silver bullet but from millions upon millions of individual face-to-face actions and transactions. Success is marked by the rebirth of hope, opportunity and freedom—hope for a better life, free from want, free from disease, free from fear. —President Kennedy, inaugural address (1960)

There is no recipe to follow to reach out to all those in poverty and help them break through its barriers. Answering the persistent and tough challenges requires a collective effort and an unwavering commitment. With no "script" for success, it calls on us to be risk takers and inventors. It asks us to refuse to succumb to the constraints of a current system that keeps perpetuating poverty.

Individual awareness of the nature of challenges faced by people in generational poverty, though a powerful first step, can never be sufficient to make long-term differences and sustainable solutions. Comprehensive organizational/systemic change, combined with committed leadership, is the only way to successfully address the complexity of the barriers faced by people in generational poverty. What we need is to transform our organizational cultures to become ones that embrace and empower people from poverty to overcome these barriers to success.

The main goal of this section is to provide general guidelines for addressing the structural barriers that keep people in poverty. It provides a road map to initiate a sustainable process of systemic change. Each organization is unique and different and each of its members has unique experiences that shape their worldview and expectations. While there are certainly best practices and solid research to rely on for impacting poverty barriers, each organization must problem-solve, understand, and create their own plans/interventions to respond to the needs of people living in poverty.

Creating Solutions from Within: Blueprints For Change

Each community has its own strengths and assets to call upon. Research on organizational change has shown that sustainable change must come from within and must be grounded in the community's vision and leadership capacity (Schein, 1992; Fullan, 2001). Therefore, there is no magic quick fix to make an organization responsive and successful in addressing the needs of people in poverty. Rather, it is an evolutionary process (as outlined below) that can lead an organization towards poverty competency.

MONO ECONOMIC EXPERIENCE

- Members of the organization act like all families are from the same economic class or culture.

- Expectation from "experts" for families to conform to the behavior and communication styles of the middle class.

- Information services are received only by complying with middle class rules and norms.

- All families are expected to "act" middle–class (be on time, have correct paperwork, participant and so on).

- Differences in resources, priorities, culture, economic opportunity, literacy and life experiences are downplayed.

NON-DISCRIMINATORY

- Attention paid to removing cultural or economic related roadblocks that inhibit families from receiving services in ways that are helpful and meaningful to them.

- An organizational goal is to increase methods of communicating and serving people in poverty situations.

- Poverty related awareness and communication training is usually offered in this stage.

- Members of the organization give a little to compromise to the needs of those with different cultural or economic backgrounds and resources.

ECONOMIC COMPETENCY

- Recognition and valuing of differences, preferences, backgrounds, opportunities and values.

- "Experts" help people from different backgrounds to navigate their system including presenting information in multiple formats and providing one-on-one coaching.

- Staff is conscious about how different experiences, perceptions and communication styles affect priorities and relationships.

- Organization staff is aware of their own perceptions about difference and able to suspend judgment of behavior, attitude, and styles that may not match their own.

- New organizational norms are created that allow for more leeway for families to participate in ways that makes the most sense to them.

- Organization policies and procedures are flexible enough to work for everyone, not just those with economic privilege.

- Poverty competency issues/barriers to information and services are openly discussed in meetings and in general in the organization.

- Staff spend time sharing success stories for helping people break down poverty-related barriers.

This change process is based in inquiry where small groups determine areas to focus on, learn about poverty, study examples of how others have responded with positive results, and generate their own goals, strategies, and solutions. The proposed solutions are continually tested, modified, refined and replaced as needed. The outline below sets the stage for initiating, planning, implementing, and evaluating the change process.

STAGE I: Preparing For Change

"The first problem for all of us, men and women, is not to learn, but to unlearn."
—Gloria Steinem

Core knowledge for building an organizational culture that is responsive to poverty conditions and the people who live in poverty

- Historical perspectives on poverty in the United States and the current conditions of people in poverty.

- Key concepts for understanding our own attitudes and beliefs as well as understanding the context of generational poverty (perception, membership, motivation, identification, and empathy).

- A recognition that motivating people in poverty requires knowing them on a personal level and knowing what is going on in their lives and what is most important to them.

- How communication and learning styles are impacted by poverty conditions (oral and print culture styles of learning, communicating, and relating).

- Familiarity with the theories of: Resiliency, Strengths Perspective, Assets, and Social Capital. Applying these theories provides a foundation for creating authentic opportunity and addressing barriers related to poverty.

- Importance of flexibility and comprehensiveness in any approach to addressing the needs of people in poverty. Design your system to serve people and remove access barriers and policies that punish people for their poverty conditions.

- An awareness of individual poverty competencies in your organization. Who has experienced poverty? Use their expertise. Who judges or does not understand? Provide training.

Examining our values, biases and assumptions related to people in generational poverty:

- How do we interpret the behavior of people in poverty?

- What misperceptions do we hold as we try to under stand the behavior, actions, and reactions of people in poverty?

- Where do we assign the "blame" for failure?

Examining the current vision and goal of your organization:

- Is moving people out of poverty part of your organizational goals?

- Does your organizational vision empower and embrace people who live in the crisis of poverty, and reflect commitment and sensitivity to the challenges they face?

Ensuring staff commitment and their readiness to engage in the change process:

- Does your staff feel the need for an intervention?

- Is your staff aware of the challenges and possibilities of serving people in poverty?

- Does the staff understand the potential impact of the change to their work?

- Does the staff understand the potential challenges that will come with embarking on the change process?

- Are moving people out of poverty strategies tied to performance reviews?

STAGE II: Action Planning Process and On-Going Evaluation

The evaluation and action planning stage are designed for integration into the organizational plans for improvement. The process is composed of three phases that are repeated as needed. The goal is to first create a current snapshot of what is working well, then customize strategies for improving success for individuals living in poverty conditions in your community/served by your organization while continuously evaluating the process and its success. The three phases are:

PHASE ONE—CAPTURING YOUR ORGANIZATION'S CURRENT REALITY: POVERTY COMPETENCY ASSESSMENT

Phase One focuses on the competency in your organization for serving individuals living in poverty conditions. It examines what your community is doing that is working well and identifies areas for growth. This process is similar to other needs assessment processes; however, the focus in the poverty competency examination is to look exclusively at the environment from the perspective of those living in poverty. This is an information-gathering phase using surveys, focus groups and interviews.

The following are assessed in Phase One:

- Existing policies and practices, e.g. spoken and unspoken/sacred cows

- Staff and leadership competencies, including individual attitudes, beliefs, skills, and values regarding children and families living in poverty

- Existing capacity of the organization to reduce/overcome poverty related barriers (what's working)

- Capacity of community partnerships and/or parent involvement to support organizational efforts to reduce poverty effects

Also in Phase One, the organization forms the Poverty Competency Advisory Team. This is a group made up of staff/leadership, parents, and community stakeholders. This team meets regularly to provide guidance and assist with assessment and the implementation of the action plan (Phase Three).

Outcomes for Phase One:

- Baseline data in the words of your staff, those you serve, and your partners showing your organization's strengths regarding serving/working with individuals who are living in poverty conditions

- Areas for improvement identified where individuals are falling through the cracks. This information serves as a tool for planning and measuring progress.

- The formation of the Poverty Competency Advisory Team.

- All staff (including advisory team members) receive poverty training.

ACTIVITY 8: POVERTY COMPETENCY ASSESSMENT

Below are critical areas to address for improving opportunities for people from poverty. Use the questions on the following page to help define each of the critical areas. Then check the box on the right that best fits the current reality of your organization. An area is ***emerging*** if there is awareness about the issue surrounding it and you have begun thinking about the issue. An area is ***developing*** if there is awareness and some attempts are being made to develop an action plan. An area is ***proficient*** if there is awareness, goals are measurable, action plans are developed, and there is some evidence that things are working well (people are seeing a difference!). An area is ***distinguished*** if there is awareness of the issues, action plans are consistently effective, and you have the ability and willingness to share your experiences/your model with others. Action plans should include aspects for addressing each of these areas.

	Emerging	Developing	Proficient	Distinguished
1. Education and Self-Awareness About Poverty and Its Causes				
2. Organizational Policies and Procedures that are Responsive to Poverty Conditions				
3. Partnerships & Resources				
4. Staff Buy-In				
5. Collaborative Relationships				
6. Effective Communication Skills (Oral culture training)				
7. All Staff as Mentors				
8. Building Resiliency and Positive Self-Concept				
9. Exposure Opportunities				
10. Maintaining Motivation/ Building Value of Education/ Planning for the Future				
11. Welcoming Families/Reaching out to the Community				

Questions to ponder as you fill out the Poverty Competency Assessment

1. Education and self-awareness about poverty and its causes: Is the history of poverty taught in your organization? Are staff members trained on poverty competencies necessary for serving those living in the context of poverty? Are poverty issues included as a topic of conversation at all staff meetings?

2. Assess organizational policies and procedures: Have you examined your organization's policies and procedures through the lens of poverty to see if they are serving those living in poverty conditions? Are they responsive to poverty conditions?

3. Partnerships and resources: Does your organization have enough community partnerships to provide a comprehensive approach to addressing barriers related to poverty (clothes, supplies, utilities, housing, food, jobs, legal help)? Do staff members know the neighborhoods/community where those from poverty live (i.e. are there sidewalks, what kinds of businesses are in their area, how are they treated in their community, what is available to them in their community)?

4. Staff buy in: Do you have staff buy-in for increasing the success of individuals living in poverty? Do you have a shared vision and clearly stated goal on how your organization will serve people in poverty?

5. Collaborative relationships: Have you begun to develop a collaborative program? Does your organization have professional development teams who discuss and share best practices for serving people in poverty? Do you help individuals form peer (helping) relationships (i.e. student-to-student, parent-to-parent)?

6. Effective communication skills (oral culture training): Does your organization have a program to address vocabulary/grammar/oral culture language differences and help individuals gain the middle class vocabulary and the skills of print culture while honoring and learning from the wealth of skills people from oral culture bring?

7. All staff as mentors: Are staff in your organization able to act as mentors (as defined by Levine and Nidiffer, and Beegle): i.e. Do they believe in the person, do they believe that there is a way out of poverty, are they aware of the history of poverty and local poverty conditions, and do they introduce those they are mentoring to people within their network? Do individuals identify with staff (e.g. Do they see how they are like them and do staff see how they are like those from poverty) For example, do staff members self-disclose personal stories and/or examples of how they learned/how they created success for themselves?

8. Building resiliency and positive self-concept: Do staff know how to build positive self-concepts among those in poverty situations? Can they remind an individual what is special about them?

9. Exposure opportunities: Do those from poverty have opportunities to become exposed to outside adventures that will increase their awareness of possibilities (e.g. trying new foods, visiting new places, and meeting professionals in a relaxed setting)?

10. Motivation/value of education/planning for the future: Can your staff help people from poverty externalize the blame and raise their awareness about the external barriers that are challenging their progress towards success? Can they make their services meaningful to them? Can they empower and motivate them to challenge those barriers and aim for success?

11. Welcoming families and reaching out to the community: Do staff know how to set up a welcoming climate for people in crisis? Do they reach out to the community to understand the social context that surrounds the people they are trying to serve?

PHASE TWO—DATA INTERPRETATION AND PRESENTATION
Phase Two consists of:

- Creating focus groups and survey data analysis
- Providing a presentation of the Poverty Competency Assessment findings
- Facilitating brainstorming sessions designed to
- Set new goals specific to the areas for growth
- Determine priorities and decide on areas to target for improvement
- Define the guidelines for necessary actions/strategies for improving outcomes for individuals living in poverty.

Outcomes for Phase Two:

- An increase in the awareness of what your organization is doing that is working.
- Actions to impact those areas identified for growth in Phase One assessment results.

PHASE THREE—FINALIZING THE ACTION PLAN
Phase Three focuses on:

- Refining actions, plans, and strategies identified in Phase Two
- Identifying necessary resources and measurable outcomes
- Identifying the role of the administration, staff, and physical environment in the proposed change
- Selecting a minimum of three staff to champion each action
- Presenting the comprehensive year-long action plan to improve success for individuals living in poverty to all stakeholders
- Forming implementation groups to ensure its successful results for people living in poverty
- Outlining a timeline for reflecting upon the results from the ongoing evaluation

Outcomes for Phase Three:

A comprehensive yearlong custom action plan to increase success for individuals living in poverty conditions. This plan is designed to be folded into the organizational improvement plan.

ACTIVITY 9: MOVING FROM WORDS TO ACTION

The task for action groups is to brainstorm challenges and identify problem areas, then start designing actions to address the challenges in each area on an on-going basis. The guidelines generated from Phases One and Two will be used as the general umbrella that provides direction and accountability criteria. Meanwhile, these guidelines are subject to revision and change based on the result of the on-going evaluation all through the implementation phase. The action plans/ problem-solving strategies generated in this process should describe the following:

Area/challenge you want to affect (i.e. attendance, motivation, parent involvement, communication, improved collaboration, partners):

Desired outcome:

Intervention strategy:

Champions (three key staff who lead the change):

Resources (fiscal, physical, and human):

Monitoring progress (How will you know it is working?):

Sample Poverty Competency Assessment and Action Plan

On the next few pages is a sample of what the Poverty Competency Assessment and Action Planning process can look like. This example is from a school, but gives a perspective for all organizations on how to promote system change that truly makes a difference for people living in poverty.

INTRODUCTION

In the 2004-2005 school year, one Oregon middle school opted to take the Poverty Competency Assessment and create a plan of action to address the educational needs of their students who live in poverty. The goal of this yearlong process was to ensure that poverty conditions did not prevent students from succeeding. In the fall of 2004, surveys were filled out by members of the school staff (including teachers, aides, staff, and administrators), students, and family members to determine strengths and barriers in educating students living in poverty. In addition to the surveys, focus group discussions were conducted with staff, family members, and students from each grade level. The data was collected to explore attitudes, beliefs, values and educational experiences related to poverty from the perspective of students, teachers and family members. In March of 2005, staff and teachers participated in brainstorming sessions to identify actions for improving educational opportunities. The following sections outline the three phases of the assessment, a partial summary of the poverty competency assessment data findings, and the action plan that was developed.

PHASE ONE—CURRENT REALITY

Phase One sought an understanding of the current learning environment at the school, examined what they were doing well/what was working, and identified areas for growth—focusing exclusively on the educational experience of students living in poverty conditions. The following areas were assessed in

Phase One:

1. Existing policies and practices—spoken and unspoken

2. Staff and leadership competencies—individual attitudes, beliefs, skills, and values regarding students and families living in poverty

3. Existing capacity of the school to reduce/overcome poverty related education barriers

4. Capacity of community partnerships/family involvement to support school efforts to reduce poverty effects

Also, in Phase One, the Poverty Advisory Team (PAT)—a group of school staff/leadership, family members, and community stakeholders who would provide oversight. This group received poverty competency training from Communication

Across Barriers. They met regularly to provide guidance and assist with the poverty competency assessment and with implementation of the action plan. PAT would be responsible for communicating the process to school leaders (who were not on the team) and to staff as the assessment and plan developed.

PHASE TWO—DATA INTERPRETATION AND PRESENTATION

Phase Two focused on interpreting the data. Survey answers were computed and open-ended questions coded and analyzed for consistent themes. As themes emerged, areas for growth were identified. After questions and clarifications, teachers and staff broke into subgroups to identify a minimum of two actions for each growth area. One PAT member served on each subgroup. They were given the data findings for a specific growth area (i.e. family involvement) and were provided with criteria for developing the action: each action had to be doable with current resources and had to be measurable.

Phase Two consisted of:

1. Analysis of focus group and survey data

2. Presentation of the findings to all staff

3. Facilitated brainstorming sessions to define actions

4. Presentation of actions to PAT

PHASE THREE—ACTION PLAN

Phase Three focused on drafting the final action plan and coordinating it with the larger organizational strategic plan. In this phase, the draft was presented to teachers, staff and PAT for a final revision and implementation. Phase Three included:

- PAT review of each action with subgroups through the lens of "Is it doable?" and "Is it measurable?"

- Scheduling subgroup meetings and PAT meetings to provide oversight for implementation.

- Final revisions to the action plan including:

- Identifying necessary resources and measurable outcomes

- Selecting champions for the efforts

- Forming work groups to ensure its successful implementation

SUMMARY OF TEACHERS' DATA

One of the most positive findings from this school was that the majority of school staff and teachers believed that students in poverty could learn with the right supports and wanted to help them succeed. In addition to believing in student's potential, the data also revealed a strong caring environment at the school. Teachers and staff showed concern that poverty was an issue that needed to be addressed. "We all recognize it as a problem, but don't have a specific resolution," wrote one teacher. Comments on caring were woven throughout the data. "This is a very caring and committed staff...they come through with all kinds of help and support. They are willing to do everything they can." When asked if students from poverty felt supported and cared for, "I hope so" was a common response. "My hope is that each student feels supported and cared about by at least one staff member. But I am sure there are some who slip through unnoticed, or at least feel that they do."

Despite the strong sense of caring and belief in students' potential, the data revealed that teachers felt they did not have all the resources they needed to achieve their goals of helping students of poverty succeed. The data revealed three main areas for growth: 1) additional time and resources, 2) increased skills, training, and knowledge of poverty, and 3) enhanced support from peers, administration, and community.

Time and resources: Data revealed that teachers wanted more time and resources to provide the extra help and encouragement that students from poverty needed to succeed. Survey results showed that only 25 percent of teachers and staff said they were always able to obtain training and resources when they needed them. Half of the teachers said they only "sometimes" had the extra time and resources needed to help students who were struggling. Only 15 percent reported knowing where to get community resources to help students and families struggling with poverty. "Time for one-on-one help, time for developing relationships with students, and resources for providing extra supports seems to be the biggest issues," was stated by one teacher. Another teacher reflected, "Teaching students who are dealing with hunger and family members in jail is very time-consuming. We never have enough time to be really effective."

Teachers showed frustration with the homework policy. One teacher said, "Several of my students in poverty consistently do not do their homework, and it is a huge battle trying to figure out what to do about it." The teacher contemplated solutions, saying, "I don't know if I should lower their grades because of it or reduce the homework for everyone so that all students are doing equal amounts of work." In open-ended and focus group data, teachers suggested ideas to help students with homework, such as smaller class sizes so they could give extra help in the classroom, volunteers to help with homework, and transportation so students could stay after school to get help.

In addition to a desire for more time to help students with homework, over half the teachers said they would also like more time to get to know their students personally. Most teachers reported that they related their own personal stories and experiences to students, but only a quarter of teachers said they knew something non-academic about each of their students. Teachers said that if they had time to learn more about their students it would help them better relate the curriculum to the lives of students. "Everyone should succeed, however if I do not know what is going on in their lives, it's hard to help."

Skills, training and knowledge of poverty: The school has provided training on educating students from poverty, but teachers reported a desire for more knowledge. More than half reported not understanding the structural causes of poverty. Over half the teachers and staff reported difficulty understanding the behavior of children and families that are struggling, and most requested opportunities to improve communication, develop a better understanding of their students behaviors, and discover strategies to alleviate the effects of poverty on learning. One teacher said, "Many of us have had training, but we could use so much more. It takes a while to really understand this complex issue." Another teacher reported, "I need to hear information on poverty multiple times to really get it."

In addition to limited knowledge on poverty, talking openly about poverty was also reported as missing. Only a small number of teachers said they discussed poverty with their students and only a third said they used examples that related to students living in poverty. Teachers said they would like to incorporate poverty issues into the classroom curriculum, but did not know how. Almost half said they would like strategies for creating a caring environment in their classroom among students of various economic backgrounds.

Survey results showed communication barriers between teachers and family members. Only 28 percent of teachers reported feeling comfortable communicating with family members/guardians living in poverty, and a third said they were not always able to suspend judgment of students and families to focus on helping students succeed. One teacher wrote, "The offer for education is there, but they don't care." Another teacher's echoed the comment by saying, "I can't understand why the parents won't do more to get their kids educated. It's as if they just don't care."

Eighty percent of teachers reported a desire to learn skills and strategies to engage family members who are living in poverty in their child's education. Data showed that many teachers were not involved with families because they did not know how to engage them and often left the task to the Parent Involvement Coordinator. When asked if family members and guardians from poverty backgrounds were involved in the learning experience, many teachers wrote "don't know," "think so" or that "happens through the parent center." Only 11 percent said they visited students' homes, while the majority of teachers (66 percent) said they did not.

Support from peers, administration and community: Teachers reported feeling overwhelmed by trying to help students living in poverty and emphasized a need for support from the school administration, colleagues, and the community. Teachers said they experienced frustration with lack of tools and strategies. They also mentioned that a lack of understanding got in the way of doing their jobs. The data and comments illustrated that a comprehensive, holistic approach and understanding by staff, administrators, teachers and community partners was needed.

Teachers reported a desire for more peer support. Even though the findings indicated a caring atmosphere among teachers and staff, they overwhelmingly reported not talking to each other about poverty issues. Most teachers said their colleagues would help them connect with students if they were having a problem, but only 31 percent reported knowing which of their fellow teachers had expertise with students living in poverty. Most teachers and staff reported a desire to know which of their colleagues lived in poverty or had experience working with students or families living in poverty. One teacher captured this theme with the comment, "I'd love to hear more success stories from my colleagues. What did they do? Then I can modify it for my class."

Teachers also reported a desire for more administrative support to help them educate students living in crisis conditions. When asked if the administration was supportive, several open-ended comments revealed that it could be improved. However, teachers showed understanding that often the lack of administrator support was due to funding issues. "Administrative support is not ideal, but it is as much as can be expected with time limitations and budget constraints." Other teachers showed less understanding with statements such as, "This school administration says they want to provide help, but then their actions speak differently." Another teacher's comment illuminated this theme with, "We need more leadership on this issue. We are often left on our own to deal with poverty issues in addition to our normal teaching requirements."

Teachers overwhelmingly reported a belief that more community support could help students living in poverty, but many revealed they had little knowledge of how much support the school received. Although the level of current support was not clear, many teachers reported a desire for stronger community partnerships. Others appeared to take a more passive role, stating that it was the administrator's job to provide teachers with knowledge about where they could get more community support. Over half said they would like an organized effort to retain additional support and believed the community would get more involved if the school was more organized. One teacher summed up this general theme by stating, "I don't even know if our community realizes how much and what kind of help we need at this school."

SUMMARY OF STUDENTS' DATA

The student survey contained questions that explored the student's relationships with teachers and their peers. Additional focus group questions examined the learning needs of students living in poverty. Results showed three main areas for growth:

1) relationship with teachers, 2) caring and safe relationships with peers, and 3) encouragement and curriculum relevant to their lives.

Relationships with teachers: Students at the school overwhelmingly reported a desire for opportunities to develop better relationships with teachers. More than half the students said when teachers did not know them it made it hard to understand where they were coming from. More than half the students reported they would like to know their teachers better and 73 percent said their teachers did not always know who they were. Several aspects of the data showed that students felt like they did not get special attention from teachers:

• 65 percent said teachers did not make them feel important

• 37 percent felt teachers did not talk to the entire class

• 35 percent reported that teachers were not always fair with them

• 28 percent said they would like to be treated with more respect

• 25 percent reported that teachers were mean, teased or yelled at students

Caring and safe relationships with peers: In addition to a theme of caring among staff and teachers, the data also showed that students cared about each other. Comments about relationships were the most common response in the open-ended data. Of this relationship category, 20 percent of the comments pertained to the desire for all students to succeed, support each other, and be happy, positive, and safe. One student wrote, "I would make sure everyone is treated fairly, and, if some people need help on their assignments, they can ask. Then we all can be honor students." Another student showed support for other students by writing, "I would make sure that everyone gets passing grades and, for the ones that don't, I would get them help!"

However, the data showed many students did not feel safe from verbal or physical abuse. Almost half (43 percent) the comments on relationships pertained to the desire for students to be nicer to each other and to teachers. Only 44 percent said that other students cared about them and more than half felt like they did not belong. One student wrote, "I would make sure that no one is being told that someone is going to beat them up." Students overwhelmingly wanted more connections and a better sense of community at the school, as expressed in one student's desire, "I wish the school was a place where every student wanted other students to succeed."

Building positive peer relationships and creating opportunities in the classroom for better understanding of different experiences was crucial to creating a safe atmosphere. Student survey results showed that the school needed more strategies to build relationships between students. Letting students share their personal experiences in the classroom is one strategy that helped students get to know each other, however, only about a third of the students said that teachers let them share. More than half the students would like opportunities to increase student participation in school activities—which they currently reported to be limited to about half the students.

Encouragement and curriculum: Over half the students reported a desire for teachers to tell them more frequently how they were doing. Only 43 percent said that teachers commented on their assignments. More than two thirds of the students wanted teachers to tell them what they were good at and not only "focus on problems."

Only half the students said they were comfortable asking questions. Students wrote about their hesitation with comments such as, "I wish a certain teacher helped me instead of getting mad at me every time I ask a question." Others wrote they sensed the teachers' frustration over having to repeat themselves. Another student pleaded in large print across the survey, "Don't talk too fast. And let us ask questions until you are sure we understand."

A critical finding of this report showed that only 22 percent of the students reported they could get help at home with school work. One student wrote, "I would like for teachers to help me out with the stuff I don't understand so I can get better grades!" Another student wrote, "Make sure that I know how to do my homework."

Sixty-seven percent of students felt disconnected from the curriculum and reported a desire for classroom activities that related better to "their real lives." More than half the students wanted to understand why education was important and 52 percent wanted more information about future careers. Students overwhelmingly said they needed to know how education made sense for them.

More than half the students (67 percent) said they wanted more opportunities for leadership. This request for more opportunities reflected the students' desire for a school environment that related more closely to their lived experiences at home. However, many students were not consciously aware that they had developed leadership skills through solving problems at home. Giving students leadership opportunities at school, in less chaotic situations that are more positive and rewards them for their efforts, allows them to realize their skills and potential to be successful. Overall, the majority (78 percent) wanted the education experience to be more active with more outside learning opportunities, such as extracurricular activities and field trips.

FAMILY MEMBERS'/PARENTS' DATA

The family assessment sought to determine how well the school was communicating with family members in poverty, if families felt welcomed, and if their life situations were accommodated for and taken into consideration with empathy and support. The assessment asked questions related to how well school policies and practices were working for them. It identified three areas for growth: 1) welcoming environment, 2) relationships with teachers and staff, and 3) help with child's learning.

Welcoming environment: Even though the majority of family members (82 percent) said they knew someone they could ask for help, less than half (43 percent) said they felt welcome at the school. One parent wrote, "Make the front office staff friendlier." In addition to staff actively welcoming family members, the data revealed that 69 percent of families wanted the school to work with them if their children were having a hard time. Another parent wanted to be welcomed and invited into the school rather than "wandering around, trying to figure out who to talk to."

Only about half the families felt like teachers cared specifically about their child. Family members overwhelmingly wanted teachers to make positive comments about their children. Of the open-ended data, 25 percent of the comments pertained to requests for "nicer teachers." About a quarter of the family members said their child did not want to attend the school. Some also reported that teachers and staff needed more training on racism. Of the 58 surveys from family members, three comments were made about racism. One parent wrote, "Make the teachers nicer and help them understand other cultures."

Many of the family members did not know how they could get involved at the school. Of the open-ended data, 79 percent of them made comments about wanting opportunities to be part of the fun school activities or performances. Families requested, "More singing and dancing performances" and "sports games that we can attend." Other family members suggested letting them know "how to contact teachers, breakfasts they could attend with their children, and ways for them to learn more about upcoming school activities."

Better communication with teachers and staff: Of the open-ended data, the most frequent comments from family members were requests for better communication with teachers and staff. One parent suggested, "Reorganize the front office to make information and access easier." Family members requested opportunities to visit and learn more about their child's learning environment. This data was consistent with the survey results that showed 71 percent of families would like more frequent information on how their child was doing at school. One parent wrote, "I want to know the minute my child is struggling, not after she has failed."

Family members also wanted to build relationships with teachers. One wrote, "I would make it so that parents meet every teacher." Survey results showed that 76 percent said they would like more information about their child's teachers. The open-ended comments contained requests for informal and fun ways to get to know the teachers. "I would like fun events to come to—activities, games, arts and crafts day."

Help with child's learning: An analysis of the data showed that family members wanted better policies and practices that accommodated their struggles, while at the same time, supported their child's learning—including a change to their home-work policies. Most (76 percent) did not want more homework for their child and said they needed the school to help more with their child's school work. They want-ed their child to receive extra assistance at school since they were often not able to help at home. Of the open-ended data, more than half the comments (76 percent) pertained to requests for "one-on-one tutoring," or "extra help" with school work. One parent wrote, "I would make sure that all the children's needs are met to make each one of them feel comfortable." Just over half the family members would like their child to receive extra help before they were failing. One parent wrote, "Teach-ers need to let family members know when students need extra help when they first start having a hard time. It is not helpful to hear every three months or so after they have failed or are too far behind." Another parent summed up this frustration with, "I didn't even know my child was failing until I got a report card at the end of the year when it was too late."

Parents care about their children's learning. Even though many did not want more homework, they did want their children to learn and succeed. Throughout the open-ended data, there were numerous requests for work that was challenging and stimulating. Family members did not want the educational standards to be lowered. One parent's commented, "I would like the school work to be more challenging, but also appropriate to my child's ability."

Family members recognized that teachers did not always have time to give extra help in the classroom. Comments were also made on class size with some fam-ily members recognizing that the large class sizes could be hurting their child's learning. In the open-ended data, more than half (65 percent) said they would like smaller class sizes. One parent wrote, "I think we need smaller class sizes so that each student gets the help they need." Family members also wanted teachers to make sure their student felt comfortable asking questions. More than half the family members (63 percent) made comments such as, "encourage students to ask ques-tions" or "make sure students understand."

The family members wanted the school to be more welcoming. Contrary to the perception that low-income families did not want to be part of the learning, these family members were requesting opportunities to be involved and to have improved communication with teachers.

ACTION PLAN

Armed with data specific to improving education for students in poverty, sub-groups began developing their plan from a strengths-based approach. The goal of the Poverty Competency Action Plan was to build on the positive qualities of the school and to work on areas where stakeholders had identified they would like to see growth. A comparison of the responses between teachers, students and family members revealed five main categories for the school staff to focus on:

1. Relationships and communication

2. Teachers' time, resources, skills, and knowledge of poverty

3. Homework policies and practices

4. Family involvement

5. Career and leadership opportunities

1. Relationships and Communication

Teacher-to-student: The most alarming analysis of the data revealed a discrepancy in the communication between teachers and students. Perceptions of caring were strikingly different. Even though 96 percent of teachers believed in their students' potential, only 35 percent of students said teachers made them feel important. Further data analysis showed that students and teachers both reported a desire for opportunities for relationship building. Teachers reported a need for more time and smaller classes or more adult help in the larger classes to build effective relationships with students. In addition, teachers wanted more resources and supports to give extra help to students living in poverty. Only about a quarter of the teachers said they knew something non-academic about each of their students. Consistently, a majority of students (74 percent) said that teachers did not know them. Through brainstorming of an action plan, teachers and staff identified one main goal with specific actions to promote growth in and create time to build rapport with students:

Goal: Teachers and staff make time to build rapport with students			
Actions	Champions	Resources	Progress
1. Teachers will eat with students in advisory classrooms (in teams of two), switching teachers every other day to create more bonding time with students 2. Change lunch; no cafe line, use kiosks to serve entire school all at the same time	• Administrators • Teachers • Cooks	Lunch serving stations (one per building)	90 days: Lunch schedule revised to allow teachers to eat with students

Student-to-student: Even though students' data showed a strong sense of caring for each other, the data also revealed that a majority of students did not feel a sense of community. In focus group data, students reported verbal and physical abuse at the school, including bullying and teasing. Data from both teachers and students showed a desire for a more positive school environment. Almost half the teachers reported they did not know how to create a caring school climate which reflected the students responses: more than half the students said that other students did not care about them; almost half felt like they did not belong at the school; half were not comfortable asking questions in the classroom; and almost half did not participate in school activities. Four goals with specific actions to improve the overall relationship building opportunities between students and improve the environment at the school were identified:

Goal: The school environment fosters relationship building and a sense of caring among students			
Actions	**Champions**	**Resources**	**Progress**
1. Crate a "Parade of Stars" spotlight featuring students, teachers, staff, and administrators that is accessible for all to see. 2. Current photos of students will be displayed. Teachers/staff will display a baby picture and a middle school picture of themselves. 3. Each person will record hobbies, favorites, talents, etc.	• Administrators • Teachers • Staff • Students • Coordinators for "Parade of Stars" hallway display	• Digital camera, or partnership with local photographer • Paper, pens, markers • Wall space to hang "Parade of Stars" displays	**30 days:** Determine which students are struggling and create schedule to make sure they are highlighted first **60 days:** Plan entire year's spotlight schedule to ensure all students, teachers, and staff are showcased by year's end

Goal: The school environment is caring and friendly			
Actions	**Champions**	**Resources**	**Progress**
Monthly school theme will be adopted to instill a sense of belonging and pride	• PAT • Administrators • One teacher from each grade level • 3 students	• Time to plan the themes • Coordinator for publicizing themes	**30 days:** Themes developed **60 days:** First 2 themes are publicized **90 days:** Students and staff are talking about and participating in themes

Goal: Student, staff, teachers, and administrators are proud of school grounds			
Actions	**Champions**	**Resources**	**Progress**
1. Teams will be organized to paint a pride mural on campus 2. Get donations for supplies from the community	• Teachers • Advisors • Students • Community volunteers	• Mural coordinators • Paint supplies	**30 days:** Obtain community donations for supplies **60 days:** Teams of interested students, staff, and community are formed **6 months:** Complete murals' exterior walls on garbage cans

Goal: Students, staff, and teachers take responsibility and pride in keeping their school clean			
Actions	**Champions**	**Resources**	**Progress**
Teams and advisories will lead students in campus clean up—rotating each week. They will create a school wide curriculum to tie in with civic and earth responsibility—establishing a clean campus as a monthly theme.	• Students • 1 teacher from each grade level • Administration • Custodial staff	• Cleaning supplies • Supervisory (teachers, administrators, and custodians)	**30 days:** Create schedule for clean up rotations **60 days:** Survey students to see if they like campus better

Teacher-to-family: Analysis of the data showed a desire for more communication and relationship building between teachers and family members. Only about a quarter (28 percent) of teachers said they were comfortable communicating with families living in poverty, and only about quarter of family members (29 percent) said they got regular information about how their child was doing. While the majority of teachers reported caring and believing in the potential of the students, only half the family members felt the teacher cared about their child. Teachers wanted actions for engaging family members in their child's education. Family members reported a desire to feel more welcomed and connected to teachers and the environment at the school. Six goals were identified to improve communication between teachers and families:

Goal: Teachers and staff have positive relationships with family members living in crisis situations			
Actions	**Champions**	**Resources**	**Progress**
1. Teachers visit/call family members early in the school year, asking how they would like to get information about how their child is doing 2. A quarterly video tape for family members will be created to show what is happening at the school 3. Administrators will endure that language issues are addressed in communications to the home—bilingual issues, non-English speaking family members, and (functionally) illiterate families/guardians	• Administrator • Teachers • Community partners • Students in video production class	• Time to visit homes • Community donations (VHS tapes) • Copy capacity for VHS tapes	**60 days:** Parents contacted **90 days:** Data given to teachers on how families want to communicate **120 days:** Video tapes completed and distributed to teachers

Goal: Teachers have frequent communication with family members			
Actions	**Champions**	**Resources**	**Progress**
1. Teachers distribute progress reports to advisory teacher every three weeks 2. Advisors make three positive contacts with family members early in the school year, letting parents know how their child is doing and how much they enjoy having them at the school 3. Family members are personally invited to school activities.	• Team Teachers (advisory, core, Explore) • Team leaders • Parents • Administrators	Advisors' time to make calls	**90 days:** Recording of number of contacts

Goal: Family members feel welcome at the school			
Actions	**Champions**	**Resources**	**Progress**
1. "Imagination Tour" of campus. Create themes of glamour, sensationalism, and exaggeration (think tabloid magazines: National Enquirer, Globe). Have students perform skits. 2. Have music playing when family members arrive. 3. Potluck dinner with main dish provided by school. 4. Games with no academic conversations.	• Parent volunteers • Front office staff • Administration • Parent Involvement Coordinator	• Funding for supplies (food and prizes) • Teacher/staff participation • Community donations and partnerships • Scheduled date for party	• **30 days:** Teachers and students share planned themes and activities • **90 days:** School is decorated with themes tied into what school stands for and what teachers love about students • Count parents in attendance

Goal: The school has simple and relaxing activities for family members to participate in			
Actions	**Champions**	**Resources**	**Progress**
1. Show movies at the school (perhaps every other Friday) 2. Invite families to watch the movie with students 3. Provide popcorn and drinks	• PAT • Administrator to obtain and coordinate snacks	• Movie rental donations from video store • Movie viewing equipment (TV/screen, VHS/DVD) • Space to watch movies • Invitations to parents	**30 days:** Collect list of family movies **6 months:** Count attendance throughout the year to measure family involvement

Goal: Activities for younger siblings are available at school functions and in the classroom			
Actions	**Champions**	**Resources**	**Progress**
1. Create activities at all functions that provide activities and supervision for younger siblings, freeing family members to participate in school functions 2. Have grab bags and prizes in classrooms for siblings to play with while teachers talk with family members 3. Recruit high school, college and community volunteers to supervise activities	• Team leader from each team • Volunteers: high school, college, community, and family members	• Coordinator • Volunteers • Designated area for sibling activities • Community support (prizes and games)	**60 days:** Recruit volunteers for yearlong functions/ Train volunteers; Solicit community support and donations **90 days:** All teachers have something for siblings to do in their class

Goal: Regularly scheduled events are available for family members to be involved at the school			
Actions	**Champions**	**Resources**	**Progress**
1. Create quarterly markets at the school campus 2. Invite students and families sell or trade crafts, art, woodwork, quilts, agriculture, etc. 3. Invite community vendors to display goods 4. Invite community entertainment 5. Let students perform/entertain (sing, play instruments, act, display art/projects)	• PAT • Administrators • Parent Volunteers • Community Volunteers • Students	• Space (outdoor or cafeteria) • Tables for display • Coordinator • Time to solicit parent and community participation	**60 days:** Community and family have re-served space **6 months:** First market happens Count how many attended

2. Teachers' Time, Resources, Skills and Knowledge of Poverty

The teachers would like more skills and knowledge for educating students living in poverty. This need was also reflected in the students' data. Many students felt disconnected from the curriculum and would like subjects that relate better to their lives. The teachers' desire to learn more skills and knowledge of poverty also emerged as a need in the family members' data. Families did not feel connected to teachers and did not feel completely welcome at the school.

Even though providing time and training was identified as one of the toughest problems to solve, teachers and staff brainstormed four goals to move forward in this area. Teachers were adamant that they needed ongoing poverty competency trainings to fully understand and have the skills and knowledge to meet the needs of their students. By satisfying teachers need for time to gain skills, other gaps were also addressed:

- Teachers would be better able to relate the curriculum to students lives, thus satisfying students needs; and

- Teaches would learn skills for connecting with family members, making them feel welcomed and engaging them in their child's learning, thus satisfying family members needs.

If successfully implemented, the four goals will improve several aspects identified as areas for growth in the poverty assessment.

Goal: Teachers have more knowledge and awareness of struggling students' neighborhoods and use the knowledge to relate to students in the classroom			
Actions	**Champions**	**Resources**	**Progress**
1. Administrators will creates a scavenger hunt in which teachers (in groups of 2-3) will visit and learn more about the neighborhoods where their struggling students live 2. Teachers will then incorporate the knowledge of neighborhoods and poverty experiences into the curriculum in a way to better connect with the students and connect the curriculum with the students' lives	• Administrator • Teachers	• Administrator time to create scavenger hunt • In-service time to do scavenger hunt	**30 days:** Administrators gather neighborhood and poverty experiences and create scavenger hunt forms **60 days:** Teachers go on scavenger hunts **6 months:** Survey teachers to see if knowledge gained is helpful in connecting them with students and relating curriculum to the student's lives

Goal: Teachers have time to learn about best practices for meeting the needs of students living in poverty conditions			
Actions	**Champions**	**Resources**	**Progress**
1. Each teacher is relieved for one day per month in order to learn more about how to meet the needs of students living in poverty 2. Administrators, classified staff, and community volunteers present information to the class (about work, skills, trades, hobbies or experiences) during the time teachers are away from the class	Administrator to coordinate schedules and recruit volunteers to present to classes	• Administrators time to present • Classified staff time to present • Community volunteers to present	**30 days:** List of community professionals to present to students **60 days:** Begin implementation of relief schedule and teachers begin focusing on gaining knowledge and skills to reduce poverty effects

Goal: Administrators provide enough support for training, skills, and resources			
Actions	**Champions**	**Resources**	**Progress**
1. Administrators seek/provide resources/training to teachers/staff for reducing the effects of poverty on learning 2. Develop a resource list for addressing poverty issues (clothing, food, housing, etc.) 3. Distribute resource list to teachers to use when helping students	• Administrator • 1 teacher from each grade level • 1 staff member • 1 parent center representative	Time to gather contacts and resources	• **60 days:** List of community resources available • **90 days:** Series of poverty-related trainings scheduled • Trainings occur and teachers provide feedback for next steps

Goal: Teachers and staff regularly share knowledge of "what works" to increase peer support for reducing the effects of poverty on learning			
Actions	**Champions**	**Resources**	**Progress**
1. Staff meets monthly to discuss successes and challenges related to students in poverty 2. Teachers rotate bringing suggestions for resources (books, articles, etc.) 3. Post "best practices" in teachers' lounge featuring successful actions (update monthly) 4. Teachers visit other classrooms to observe different teaching and learning actions	• Administrators • 1 teacher from each grade level	• Time on agenda to discuss poverty related successes and challenges • Space for posting best practices • Scheduling relief time for visiting other classes	**30 days:** Review agendas to ensure time is allocated for discussing poverty successes and challenges **60 days:** Compile a list of recommended books, articles, and resources **90 days:** Compile a list of how many teachers have visited other classrooms

3. Homework Policies and Practices

Data analysis showed that homework policies and practices were barriers for teachers, family members and students. Teachers wanted more homework to be completed while family members and students wanted less homework given. Teachers said they did not have time to give extra help on homework, while family members reported a desire for the school to provide the help they were unable to give their children at home. Many students said they were not able to get help for their homework from anyone.

Overall, students, teachers and family members agreed that students living in the context of poverty may need extra help to succeed. However, evidence from the teachers' data showed that time and resources were barriers. Both teachers and family members requested extra help in the classroom and smaller class sizes. Staff and teachers have identified a strategy to improve one-on-one help to students by soliciting and training volunteers for classroom assistance. Teachers and staff have identified five goals and nine action items to address this area:

Goal: Create a homework policy that is flexible and meets the needs of all students			
Actions	**Champions**	**Resources**	**Progress**
1. Review current policy and practices to ensure that they set students up for success and allow flexibility to meet the needs of students living in crisis conditions 2. Poverty Advisory Team makes and provides recommendations to all staff for improving homework policies and practices	Poverty Advisory Team (PAT)	• Time for teachers to submit (anonymously) current policy and practices • A scheduled date/ room for PAT to present recommendations for homework policies and practices for teachers	**2 weeks:** Teachers submit current policy and practices **90 days:** Recommendations from PAT presented to all staff **6 months:** Teachers report on: a) what changes were made based on recommendations b) Improvement in struggling students grades/work completion c) what suggestions they have for making homework policy and procedures more effective

Goal: Create options for students who struggle to finish homework at school			
Actions	**Champions**	**Resources**	**Progress**
1. Struggling students are "selected" to participate in during-school homework/ learning help 2. Students are rewarded with special privileges (food, activities, special guests) for participating in homework options	• Administrator • 1 teacher per grade level	• Space/ room • Food and rewards	**90 days:** Homework options program available **6 months:** Survey students to ask if it is helping **9 months:** Improved academic success for participating students

Goal: Ensure that students are not overloaded with homework			
Actions	**Champions**	**Resources**	**Progress**
Teachers meet monthly to collaborate on outcomes desired by homework assignments and determine in-school supports for achieving the outcomes	Teachers	Scheduled time for monthly homework meetings	**90 days:** Teachers provide examples of coordinating homework and cross curriculum efforts

Goal: Ensure family members have knowledge about and support for helping their children with homework			
Actions	**Champions**	**Resources**	**Progress**
If homework is given, family members receive a bright-colored flier with their child's photo (to catch their attention) with visual step-by-step instructions (very little text) and information on who to call or talk to for more help	• Administrators to create templates • Teachers to implement strategy	• Digital camera • Administrator time to create templates with student's photo and name	• **30 days:** Template developed • **60 days:** Photos taken, multiple fliers printed and ready for teacher use • Parent focus group to see if new policy and practices are helpful

Goal: Students receive one-on-one help with their homework			
Actions	**Champions**	**Resources**	**Progress**
1. Gather data from teachers to find out what they need from volunteers in the classroom 2. Solicit volunteers to help in the classroom from the community, high school, and colleges 3. Train classroom volunteers	• 1 teacher from each grade level • Administrator • Poverty Advisory Team	• Coordinator • Time to train • Space for training	**30 days:** Teachers submit top three wish list for volunteer's knowledge **60 days:** 50 volunteers recruited **90 days:** Volunteers are trained based on teachers' wish list and working in the classroom

4. Family Involvement

A cross analysis of data showed that teachers would like family members to be more engaged in their child's learning, and family members consistently reported feeling disconnected from the school and would like to be more involved. Furthermore, teachers reported not knowing how to communicate with people living in poverty and some admitted they were often not able to withhold judgment of the behavior of parents who were not involved with their child's learning. Family members felt that teachers did not care about their child and were often, "not nice" and did not know of easy ways they could be involved at the school.

Teachers and staff identified six strategies (as outlined in the Teacher-to-Family Relationship Building section) to improve the relationships between teachers and family members, and thus engage families in their child's learning. These strategies included increasing contact with family members and increasing the ways they communicated with family members—creating regularly scheduled and informal, easy-to-engage-in, fun activities to make families feel welcome, and providing assistance with younger siblings to give family members opportunities to participate in school activities.

5. Career and Leadership Opportunities

To help students from poverty learn, they need curriculum that relates to their lives. Many students are forced to grow up fast and often take on adult roles at a young age. Thus, many of them already have leadership experiences that were not realized or recognized by themselves or educators. The data showed that the environment at the school did not have enough opportunities for students to be recognized for their leadership abilities. Both students and family members reported a desire for more challenging opportunities for students to learn and to gain experience in leadership.

Teachers and students both expressed a desire for students to learn more about career opportunities. Students wanted to see a connection between the knowledge they were learning and how they could use the knowledge in the real world. "I need to know why school is important to me," was a comment frequently heard from the students. Teachers and staff identified two goals to improve the career and leadership opportunities for students:

Goal: Students are aware of career opportunities			
Actions	**Champions**	**Resources**	**Progress**
1. Coordinate two to three career fairs throughout the year set up like a carnival or flea market with lots of interaction opportunities 2. Highlight professions on a bulletin board with personal profiles of someone who does that work 3. Bring professionals to the classroom to talk to students about their life stories and what they do on a daily basis for their profession 4. Take students on field trips 5. Provide job shadow opportunities	• PAT • Career Center Representative • Workforce Representative • Explore Team • Parent Volunteers • Professional Volunteers	• Coordinators: teachers, parents, volunteers • Transportation for field trips • Space for bulletin boards • Space for career fair	**30 days:** Monthly careers to be spotlighted are chosen; and professionals are identified **60 days:** Several commitments from professionals; Two career field trips are planned
Goal: Students have many leadership opportunities			
Actions	**Champions**	**Resources**	**Progress**
1. Create "Explore Leadership" opportunities 2. Create Leadership Club 3. Create committees for socials, assemblies run by students 4. Select students from poverty backgrounds to lead/organize socials and assemblies	• Administrators • Students	• Supplies/community donations • High school volunteers • Hire a teacher	**30 days:** Struggling students are selected and encouraged to participate in leadership activities **90 days:** Count attendance in student leadership clubs and on committees

SUMMARY

This sample action plan shows how important it is to look at multiple levels of an organization (leadership, policy, staff, community partners, family members, students, etc.) in order to truly make a difference for people who live in poverty. It is essential to include all stakeholders in the assessment and action planning process so that all buy into the process and have ownership in the outcomes of the action plan.

Once you start to implement your action plan, the actions must be reviewed every 90 days to measure if they are working, identify areas that need refining, and rework the actions to ensure they are making a difference. Finally, the poverty competency action plan has to be folded into the larger organizational strategic plan in order to be taken seriously.

Leadership for Change

Leadership for serving people from poverty requires a comprehensive approach, a long-term commitment, and a daily focus on the vision of helping people in crisis succeed. It requires setting a tone that eradicating poverty barriers is an organizational goal and not a fad that is going away. Poverty issues must be examined in all work carried out. All aspects of the organization must be examined to ensure a holistic approach to address the barriers faced by people living in poverty conditions. Leadership that is responsive to poverty issues is a leadership that is built on two major assumptions:

1. Cultural knowledge, unique characteristics, and the intellectual potential of all regardless of social class are valued.

2. While it is very important to help people from poverty learn the knowledge, attitudes, and skills required for success in the "dominant culture," this should be done in a context of profound respect for the unique strengths they bring to the experience.

3. It is equally important to learn strengths that students and families bring and provide opportunities to welcome and highlight these strengths (loyalty, resourcefulness, creativeness, survival skills).

Fifteen essential elements for leaders to consider for providing genuine opportunities for success for those living in poverty conditions:

• Transmit clear messages from leadership that improving the situations for those living in poverty is a priority that is not going away. Include poverty-related discussions on all staff meeting agendas. Model characteristics you want to see in your staff.

• Examine and align organizational policies and procedures to ensure they are relevant and appropriately related to the lived experiences of individuals from poverty.

• Become familiar with existing policies, finding ways to interpret them in a way that serves rather than punishes people from poverty.

- Review practices to ensure that the needs of individuals with oral culture learning styles are met.

- Organize environment/activities to increase relationship-building opportunities among children, parents, staff, and leadership.

- Rally help from the community and build solid strong support for this effort. It is very important for leaders to do their homework on all the available agencies/resources in the community that can help with poverty-related barriers (such as housing, food, clothing, transportation, etc.).

- Ensure "buy in" from the staff. Build a core group among your colleagues and employees of those who are enthusiastic and willing to help drive the change.

- Raise staff awareness about the nature of the challenges that individuals from poverty face and provide professional development opportunities specifically focused on best practices for serving those living in poverty. Create internal opportunities for staff to share "what worked" or success stories.

- Set aside some time for staff to positively connect with the families they serve whether or not they seek information from your organization. The focus should be on learning about the person (e.g. What is she/he interested in? What helps her/him when he or he is frustrated?). It is easier to customize the situation when you understand the specific current reality a person is facing and what she or he believes is possible.

- Make sure that staff members set high goals for those in poverty and that they provide extra help to ensure individuals are able to overcome their specific challenges and achieve those goals.

- Evaluate those goals. Always ask, "Am I setting them up for success with the poverty conditions they face?"

- Reflect regularly as a staff on what works and what does not work for those living in poverty conditions. Collect and present frequent data on progress. Use the data to intervene early. Do not let those in poverty get behind and discouraged. Also, seek feedback on what worked and what did not, and always ask what those individuals need from you to be successful.

- Be articulate about your organization's current reality regarding serving those who are living in poverty conditions. Share data as well as anecdotes that show what you are doing, what is working, and areas in which you would like to see growth.

- Choose areas to target for improvement, and make sure the change effort addresses structure, assumptions and beliefs, human relations as well as the political aspect of your organization.

- Develop a poverty competency action plan with measurable goals.

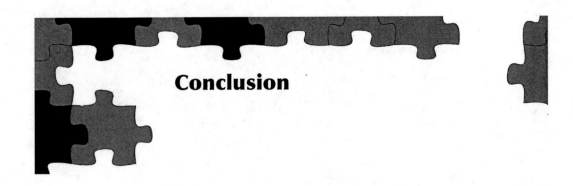

Conclusion

"It is a world of 'it's who you know'. When you are in poverty, everyone you know is segregated and also struggling. Chances are you know someone who can help someone living in poverty. Every person can be the difference. What you have in your hands can really change lives."—Dr. Donna Beegle

The goal of my work is to make a difference for people who live in poverty. I want everyone to have true opportunities to lead full lives and to reach their potential. Below are key points to keep in mind that can guide and empower you to be the difference in the lives of people living in poverty.

1. The context of poverty teaches people a worldview that is different than the context of middle-class or wealthy people. We have to meet people where they are and expose them to possibilities that are provided naturally in a middle class context.

2. Poverty is often internalized as a personal deficiency. If people do not get strong messages that there are good things about them, they may not see hope or opportunity.

3. Behaviors and values are a product of the social context in which we live and not necessarily reflective of the "kind of person" we are. As professionals, we need to suspend judgment and assume that people are making the very best decisions they can in their context.

4. Developing empathy for the experience of living in crisis situations, and respect for the strength and resourcefulness that comes because of it, are the first steps toward understanding the life conditions of people in poverty and effectively responding to their needs.

5. What you have to do to help people move out of poverty may not be in your job title, and you may not have been taught what to do in your education. Professionals must be clear about why they are doing the work they are doing. If you are clear your work is to help people move forward, you are likely to do the right thing.

6. Be vocal, motivated, and committed to become a part of or a driving force towards transformative change to achieve equity and social justice and eradicate the causes of poverty.

7. Realize that there is no easy way to achieve our goals. There is no "one thing" or "magic fix" for the complexities of poverty. The key to sustainable change lies in you and your ability to challenge the status quo and recreate a new paradigm for working with people in poverty that is inclusive, compassionate, supportive and long-term.

8. Social class should be used as a conceptual lens through which we examine and challenge our organizations, beliefs, values, and practices.

9. Discussing the systemic causes of poverty will empower those in poverty by helping them to externalize the blame. It will also open possibilities for effective change toward eradicating poverty.

10. Attention should be brought to structural inequalities, ineffective public policy, and outside barriers to opportunities.

11. Every person who works with people living in poverty must be clear about the following:

   • The goal of their work should be to help people in poverty succeed, move forward, and grow as individuals; not just be able to "cope" with their conditions

   • Growing up in poverty does cause pain, and the environment impacts a person's ability to develop to his or her full potential. However, it does not leave a "deficient" person who needs to be fixed or compensated for, but rather a person with a set of skills and strengths that equip them to face the demands of life.

   • Our effects to help should be based on the assumption that people living in poverty can, like everybody else, achieve big dreams and strive for excellence; if only we meet them where they are and link them into support networks.

   • Effective help requires building partnerships, creating support systems, and eradicating existing systemic barriers. It does not mean lowering expectations.

12. When serving those in poverty, individuals need to continually ask questions about contexts and experiences related to poverty so that they can keep learning and growing. They need to break away from past ways of thinking and doing things that often don't work. They need to find the positive examples out there that do work, think about why they worked, and adapt those principles to their own situations.

   • Spreading the word: raising collective awareness and acknowledgement of the problem of poverty.

- Questioning our current views and reconstructing our understanding based on new assumptions that are unbiased, non-judgmental and more empathetic.

- Starting from within:

  - Changing ourselves, "Be the change you want to bring to the world" —Ghandi

  - Changing our organizations by becoming change agents

  - Changing our society by being part of a group of visionaries working toward a more just world

Use this information to promote dialogue and action.

Anyon, J. (2005). What "counts" as educational policy? Notes toward a new paradigm. *Harvard Educational Review,* 75(1), 65-88.

Auletta, K. (1983). *The under class.* New York, NY: Vintage.

Bane, M., & Ellwood, D. T. (1994). *Welfare realities: From rhetoric to reform.* London: Harvard University Press.

Barnett, W.S., Hustedt, J.T., Robin, K.B., and Schulman, K.L. (2004). *2004 State Preschool Yearbook.* The National Institute for Early Education Research. Available online at: http://nieer.org/yearbook/pdf/yearbook.pdf

Beegle, D. (2003). Overcoming the silence of generational poverty. *Talking Points:* National Council of Teachers of English www.ncte.org

Beegle, D. (2000) *Interrupting generational poverty: Factors influencing successful completion of the bachelor's degree.* Doctoral Dissertation, Portland State University.

Berliner, D. (2005). Presidential invited speech to the American Educational Research Association meeting in Montreal, Canada, May, 2005. *Teachers College Record,* www.tcrecord.org, ID Number: 12106, Date Accessed: 12/31/2005 1:46:09 PM.

Benard, B. (1994, December). Applications of resilience. Paper presented at a conference on the Role of Resilience in Drug Abuse, Alcohol Abuse, and Mental Illness, Washington, DC.

Benard, B. (1997). Fostering resiliency in children and youth: Promoting protective factors in school. In D. Saleebey (Ed.), *The strengths perspective in social work practice* (2nd ed.) (pp. 167-181). New York, NY: Longman Publishers.

Bourdieu, P., & Wacquant, L. (1992). *An invitation to reflexives sociology.* Chicago, IL: University Press.

Brantlinger, E. A. (2003). *Dividing classes: How the middle class negotiates and rationalizes school advantage.* New York, NY: Routledge Falmer.

Burke, K. (1969). *A rhetoric of motives.* Berkeley, CA: University of California Press.

Coleman, J. S. (1988). Social capital in the creation of human capital. *American Journal of Sociology,* 94 (Supplement), S95-120.

Cookson, P. W., and Persell, C. H. (1985). *Preparing for power: America's elite boarding schools.*

Cooperrider, D. L. (2000). *Appreciative inquiry: Rethinking human organization toward a positive theory of change*. IL: Stipes Publishing L.L.C.

Ehrenreich, B., Hochschild, A., & Kay, S. (Eds.). (April 2002). *Nickel and dimed: On (not) getting by in America*. 1ST OWL.

Freedman, M. (1993). *The kindness of strangers : Adult mentors, urban youth and the new voluntanism*. San Francisco, CA: Jossey-Bass Publishers.

Freire, P. (1970). *Pedagogy of the oppressed*. New York: Continuum Press.

Fullan, M. (1999). *Change forces: The sequel*. Philadelphia, PA: Falmer Press.

Fulford, R. (1994). *Ong's orality and literacy: A rhetorical analysis of social class*. Paper presented at the Speech Communication Association meeting, New Orleans, LA.

Gans, H. (1995). *The war against the poor*. New York, NY: Basic Books.

Gilbert, D, Wright, M., and Jucha, B. (2003). *The American class structure in an age of growing inequality* (6th edition). Belmont, CA: Wadsworth Publishing Company.

Gill, D. (1992). *Unraveling social policy*. Rochester, VT: Schenkman Books, Inc.

Greenberg, M., Strawn, J., & Plimpton, L. (1999). *State opportunities to provide access to postsecondary education under TANF*. Washington, DC: Center For Law and Social Policy.

Grusky, D. B. (2001). *Social stratification: Class, race, and gender in sociological perspective* (2nd edition). Greeley, CO: Westview Printing.

Guba, E., & Lincoln, Y. (1989). *Fourth generation evaluation*. CA: Sage Publication.

Hamilton, S. F. (1991). *Unrelated adults in adolescent lives*. Occasional Paper No 29, New York, NY: Cornell University.

Hammond, A. (2005). The federal poverty line must be reformed. Retrieved August 7, 2006, from Chicago Maroon Online Edition. Web site: http://maroon. uchicago.edu/viewpoints/articles/2005/11/14/the_federal_poverty_.php

Heider, F. (1958). *The psychology of interpersonal relations*. New York, NY: Wiley.

Herrera, C. (1999). *A first look into its potential*. Philadelphia, PA: Public/Private Ventures.

Higgins, G. O. (1994). *Resilient adults: Overcoming a cruel past*. San Francisco, CA: Jossey-Bass.

Jarchow, C. (2002). *Employment experiences of former TANF recipients*.

Jones, T. (1998). Life after Proposition 209: Affirmative action may be dying, but the dream lives on. *Academe, 84*(4), 23-28.

Jones, E. E., Kannouse, D. E., Kelley, H. H., Nisbett, R. E., Valins, S., and Weiner, B. (Eds.). (1972). *Attribution: Perceiving the causes of behavior.* Morristown, NJ: General Learning Press.

Jordan, J. V. (1992). Relational resilience. Paper presented as part of the Colloquium Series at Wellesley College, Wellesley, MA.

Knapp, Mark (1984). *Interpersonal communication and human relationships.* Boston, MA: Allyn and Bacon.

Koball, H. and Douglas-Hall, A. (2004). *The effects of parental education on income.* The National Center for Children in Poverty.

Kretzmann, J. P. & McKnight, J. L. (1993). *Building communities from the inside out: A path toward finding and mobilizing a community's assets.* Evanston, IL: Institute for Policy Research.

Krovetz, M. (1999). *Fostering resiliency: Expecting all students to use their minds and hearts well.* Thousand Oaks, CA: Corwin Press.

Lerner, H. G., Ph.D. (1989). *The dance of intimacy: A woman's guide to courageous acts of change in key relationships.* New York, NY: Harper and Row.

Levine, A., & Nidiffer, J. (1996). *Beating the odds: How the poor get to college.* San Francisco, CA: Jossey-Bass Inc.

Lewis, D. A., Collins, E. & Amsden, L. (2005). Who gets ahead? Work profiles of former welfare recipients in Illinois. Illinois Family Study, Policy Brief, www.mcic.org

Lewis, O. (1975). The children of Sanchez. Harper Collins Publishers.

Loewin, J.W. (1995). *Lies my teacher told me: Everything your American textbook got wrong.* New York, NY: Touchstone.

London, H. B. (1992, Winter). Transformations: Cultural challenges faced by first-generation students. First-Generation Students: Confronting the Cultural Issues, 80, 5-12.

Maslow, A. (1943). A theory of human motivation. *Psychological Review*, 50, 370-396. Retrieved August 2006, from http://psychclassics.yorku.ca/Maslow/motivation.htm.

McLaughlin, M., Irby, M., & Langman, J. (1994). *Urban sanctuaries: Neighborhood organizations in the lives and futures of inner city youth.* San Francisco, CA: Jossey-Bass.

Mortenson, T. (1991). *Equity of higher education opportunity for women, Blacks, Hispanics, and low-income students* (ACT Student Financial Aid Research Report Series). Iowa City: American College Testing Program.

Mortenson, T. (Ed.). (1993). *Postsecondary education opportunity: The Mortenson report on public policy analysis of opportunity for postsecondary*. Iowa City: American College Testing Program.

Mortenson, T. (1995). *Postsecondary education opportunity: The Mortenson report on public policy analysis of opportunity for postsecondary education*. Iowa City: American College Testing Program. (ERIC Document Reproduction Service No. ED 390 368)

Mortenson, T. (1996). *Postsecondary education opportunity: The Mortenson report on public policy analysis of opportunity for postsecondary education*. Iowa City: American College Testing Program. (ERIC Document Reproduction Service No. ED 390 368)

Mortenson, T. (1998, July/August). A conversation about diversity. *Academe*, 84(4), 42-43.

Myrdal, G. (1962). *Challenge to affluence: The emergence of an under-class*. New York, NY: Pantheon Books.

Ong, W. (1982). *Orality and literacy: The technologizing of the world*. London: Methuen & Co., Ltd.

Pascale, R., Milleman, M., & Gioja, L. (2000). *Surfing the edge of chaos: The laws of nature and the new laws of business*. New York, NY: The Three River Press.

Piercy, K., Wolfe, L., & Gittell, M. (1998, August 13). Welfare rules must let women attend college. *The Oregonian*, p. B11.

Pitts Jr., L. (2006, January 15). King will want us to know that poverty does not discriminate. *The Miami Herald*.

Putnam, R. D. (1995). Tuning in, tuning out: The strange disappearance of social capital in America. PS: *Political Science and Politics*, 29, 664-683.

Richardson, R., & Bender, L. (1986). *Students in urban settings: Achieving the baccalaureate degree*. Washington, DC: The George Washington University. (ERIC Document Reproduction Service No. ED 284 518)

Rubin, L. (1976). *Worlds of pain*. New York, NY: Basic Books.

Saleebey, D., (1997). *The strengths perspective in social work practice* (2nd ed.). New York, NY: Longman Publishers.

Schein, E. (1992). *Organizational culture and leadership* (2nd Ed). CA: Jossey Bass.

Schorr, L.B. (1988). *Within our reach: Breaking the cycle of disadvantage*. New York, NY: Doubleday.

Senge, P. (1990). *The fifth discipline: The art and practice of the learning organization*. New York, NY: Currency Doubleday

Sheehy G. (1986, April 20). The victorious personality. *New York Times Magazine*, p. 26.

The Search Institute (1990). *The troubled journey: A portrait of 6th-12th grade youth.*

Smeeding, T.M. (2003). *The poverty quagmire.* Washington Post Online.

Tiger, L. and Fox, R. (1971). *The imperial man.* Holt Rinehart and Winston: New York, NY.

UNICEF (2005). *Child poverty in rich countries,* 2005. Innocenti Report Card No. 6. Florence, Italy: UNICEF Innocenti Research Centre. Retrieved May 16, 2005 from: www.unicef.org/irc and www.unicef-irc.org

United States Department of Commerce, Bureau of the Census. (2003). *Statistical abstract of the United States.* Washington, DC: Author.

United States Department of Commerce, Bureau of the Census. (2005). *Statistical abstract of the United States.* Washington, DC: Author.

Vaillant, G. E. (1993). *The wisdom of the ego.* Cambridge, MA: Harvard University Press.

Valadez, J. R. (1998, June). Applying to college: Race, class, and gender differences. *Professional School Counseling,* 1(5), 14-20. (ERIC Document Reproduction Service No. EJ 574 990)

Weber, M. (1946). *Essays in sociology* (H. H. Gerth & C. Wright Mills Eds and Trans.). New York, NY: Oxford University Press.

Weiner, B. (1986). *An attributional theory of motivation and emotion.* New York, NY: Springer-Verlag.

Wilson, W. (1987). *The truly disadvantaged: The inner city, the underclass and public policy.* Chicago, IL: The University of Chicago Press.

Wilson, W. (1996). *When work disappears: The world of the new urban poor.* New York, NY: Alfred A. Knopf, Inc.

Wolin, S. J., & Wolin, S. (1993). *The resilient self: How survivors of troubled families rise above adversity.* New York, NY: Villard.

Recommended Readings and Web Sites

Understanding Poverty, General Background

Adler, R., & Rodman, G. (1991). *Understanding human communication.* Orlando: Holt, Rinehart and Winston, Inc.

Bourdieu, P. (1974). Cultural reproduction and social reproduction. In R. Brown (Ed.), *Knowledge, education, and cultural change* (pp. 241-258). London: Harper and Row.

Bourdieu, P. (1986). The forms of social capital. In J. S. Richardson(Ed.), *The handbook of theory and research for the sociology of education* (pp. 241-258). New York: Greenwood Press.

Childers, M., & Hooks, B. (1990). A conversation about race and class. In M. Hirsh & E. Fox Keller (Eds.), *Conflicts in feminism* (pp. 60-81). NewYork: Routledge, Inc.

Collins, R. (1971). Functional and conflict theories of educational stratification. *American Sociological Review*, 36, 1002-1019.

Danziger, S., and Haveman, R. (Eds.) (2001). Understanding poverty. Russell Sage Foundation; Harvard

Darling, S. (1988, September). *Children in poverty: So what? Momentum*, p. 2. University Press: Cambridge, MA.

Davis, K., & Moore W. E. (1945). Some principles of stratification. American Sociological Review, 10(2), 242-249.

DeSouza, B. X. (1998). Brown kids in White suburbs: Housing mobility and the many faces of social capital. *Housing Policy Debate,* 9(1), 177-221.

Edwards, B., & Foley, M. W. (1997). Social capital and the political economy of our discontent. *American Behavioral Scientist,* 40, 669-678.

Ferman, A. L. (1965). *Poverty in America: A book of readings.* Ann Arbor: The University of Michigan Press.

Foley, D. E. (1990). Learning capitalist culture: *Deep in the heart of Tejas. Philadelphia:* University of Pennsylvania Press

Harrington, M. (1993). *The Other America : Poverty in the United States.* Touchstone Book: New York: NY

Kohn, M. (1969). *Class and conformity.* Homewood, IL: Dorsey Press

Koltlowitz, A. (1992). *There are no children here: The story of two boys growing up in the other america.* Anchor Books, New York: NY

Kozol, J. (1988). *Rachel and her Children: Homeless Families in America*. Fawcett Columbine: NEW York: NY.

Kozol, J. (1991) *Savage Inequalities: Children in America's School*. Harper Perennial New York: NY

Olson, D.R. & Torrance, N. (Eds.) (1991) *Literacy and Orality*. Cambridge University Press: Cambridge.

Ryan, W. (1992). Blaming the victim. In P. Rothenberg (Ed.), *Race, class, and gender in the United States: An integrated study* (pp. 364-373). New York: St. Martin's Press, Inc.

Waxman, C. I. (1983). *The stigma of poverty: A critique of poverty theories and policies*. New York: Pergamon Press.

Poverty and Education: Barriers and Possibilities

Anyon, J. (1997). *Ghetto schooling: A political economy of urban school reform*. New York: Teachers College Press.

Attinasi, L. (1989). *Getting in: Mexican American's perceptions of university attendance and the implications for freshman persistence*

Bowles, S., & Gintis, H. (1976). *Schooling in a capitalist America: Educational reform and the contradictions of economic life*. New York: Basic Books, Inc

Brint, S., & Karabel, J. (1989). *The diverted dream: Community colleges and the promise of educational opportunities in America 1900-1975*. New York: Oxford University Press.

Cabrera, A., Castaneda, M., Nora, A., & Hengstler, D. (1990, November). The convergence between two theories of college persistence. Paper presented at the annual meeting of the Association for the Study of Higher Education, Portland, Oregon.

Chaffee, J. (1992, Winter). Transforming educational dreams into educational reality. *First-Generation Students: Confronting the Cultural Issues*, 80, 81-88

Dougherty, K. J. (1992, March/April). Community colleges and baccalaureate attainment. Journal of Higher Education, 63(2), 188-214.

Featherman, D. L., & Hauser, R. (1978). *Opportunity and change*. New York: Academic Press

Rist, R. C. (1970). Student social class and teachers: Expectations: The self-fulfilling prophecy in ghetto education. *Harvard Educational Review*, 40, 411-450.

Change Perspectives: Approaches toward equity and social justice

Abdullah, S. (1999). Commons café social-class training model. (Available from S. Abdullah, 5018 N. Williams Portland, OR 97217 or www.commonwayinstitute. com)

Anyon, J. (2005). *Radical possibilities: Public policy, urban education, and a new social Movement.* Routledge: New York: NY

Abdullah, S. (1999). *Creating a world that works for all.* Portland, OR: Berrett-Koehler Publishers.

Abdullah, S. (1999). *The power of one: Authentic leadership in turbulent times. Portland, OR: Berrett-Koehler Publishers.*

Adams, M., Bell, L.A., and Griffin, P. (eds,) (1997). *Teaching for diversity and social justice: A sourcebook.* New York, NY: Routledge.

Blank, R. (1997). *It takes a nation: A new agenda for fighting poverty.* Russell Sage Foundation; Princeton University Press: Princeton, NJ.

Glasser, W. (1968). *Schools without failure.* New York: Harper and Row.

Miller, L. S. (1995). *An American imperative: Accelerating minority educational advancement.* New Haven, CT: Yale University Press.

Rethinking Schools (1994). *Rethinking our classrooms: Teaching for equity and justice. Volume 1.* Milwaukee, WI

Rethinking Schools (1994). *Rethinking our classrooms: Teaching for equity and justice. Volume 2.* Milwaukee, WI

Tomlinson, S. (1999). *The differentiated classroom: Responding to the needs of all learners.* Alexandria, VA: ASCD

Tomlinson, S. (2003). *Fulfilling the promise of the differentiated classroom: Strategies and tools for responsive teaching.* Alexandria, VA:ASCD

Tomlinson, C. A., & Allan S. D. (2000). *Leadership for differentiating schools and classrooms.* ASCD; Alexandria: VA

Waber, B (1963). *Rich Cat, Poor Cat.* Scholastic Book Services, New York: NY

Woolcock, R. (1988). Social capital and economic development: Toward a theoretical synthesis and policy framework. *Theory and Society,* 27, 151-208.

Multicultural Education

Banks, J.A. (1997). *Educating citizens in a multicultural society*. Teachers College Press: New York: NY

Banks, J.A. (ed.) (1996). *Multicultural education, transformative knowledge, and action: Historical and contemporary perspectives*. NY: Teachers College Press.

Banks, J.A. (1994) *An Introduction to multicultural education*. Boston: Allyn and Bacon

Banks, J.A. (1988). *Multiethnic education: Theory and practice, 2nd edition*. Boston: Allyn and Bacon, Inc., 1988.

Banks, C. A. M., & Banks, J. A. (1989). *Multicultural education: Issues and perspectives*. Boston: Allyn and Bacon, Inc., 1989.

Delpit, L. (1995). *Other people's children: Cultural conflict in the classroom*. The new Press, New York, NY.

Diller, J. V. & Jean Moule (2005). *Cultural competence: A primer for educators*. Thomson Wadsworth: Belmont: CA.

Web Sites

Appreciative Inquiry—David L. Cooperrider: www.12manage.com/methods_cooperrider_appreciative_inquiry.html

Communication Across Barriers: Donna Beegle's Web site which is dedicated to improving opportunities for people from generational poverty. www.combarriers.com

Institute for Research on Poverty: IRP is a center for interdisciplinary research into the causes and consequences of poverty and social inequality in the United States. www.irp.wisc.edu In addition, Poverty Dispatch Weekly is a free e-mail service of the IRP that sends a message twice a week with a dozen links to media articles with a focus on poverty, welfare reform, child welfare, health, Medicaid from across the U.S. www.canadiansocialresearch.net/povdispatchweek.htm

Learning Organizations, Five Disciplines – Peter Senge: www.12manage.com/methods_senge_five_disciplines.html and www.infed.org/thinkers/senge.htm

Positive Deviance—Richard Tanner Pascale and Jerry Sternin: www.12manage.com/methods_pascale_positive_deviance.html

Postsecondary Education OPPORTUNITY: The Mortenson Research Seminar on Public Policy Analysis of Opportunity for Postsecondary Education. www.postsecondary.org/home/default.asp

PovertyBridge: A non-profit foundation dedicated to improving opportunities for people who live with the trauma inflicted by poverty conditions. Its goals are to provide life-changing information that shatters common myths and stereotypes about people who live in poverty; offer research based strategies for improving relationships, communication, and educational success for people who live in poverty; and share ideas for advocating for people who live in poverty. www.povertybridge. org

Poverty USA: The Catholic Campaign for Human Development (CCHD) is helping American residents break free from poverty. Since it was established in 1970, CCHD has assisted people to rise out of poverty through empowerment programs that foster self-sufficiency. Each year CCHD distributes national grants to more than 300 community-based projects that improve neighborhoods, educate children, create jobs, and more. In addition, hundreds of smaller projects have helped low-income people to change their lives by creating opportunity where none existed before and providing the means for poor people to find solutions to their community's problems. www.usccb.org/cchd/povertyusa/

Grassroots Approaches to Social Justice Education

Groups include: Chicago Teachers for Social Justice, Literacy for Social Justice Teacher Research Group (St. Louis), New York Collective of Radical Educators, Portland Area Rethinking Schools, Teachers for Social Justice (SF), Education not Incarceration (Oakland), Coalition for Educational Justice (LA), and Puget Sound Rethinking Schools.

Projects supporting grassroots educator groups:

Common Way is an inclusive social change organization, dedicated to creating a society that works for all. Our goal is to foster inclusive, sustainable human societies on an ecologically viable planet. www.commonway.org

EdChange is dedicated to diversity, equity, and justice in schools and society. We act to shape schools and communities in which all people, regardless of race, gender, sexual orientation, class, (dis)ability, language, or religion, have equitable opportunities to achieve to their fullest. www.edchange.org

Facing History Ourselves helps students find meaning in the past and recognize the need for participation and responsible decision-making. It is based on the belief that students must know not only the triumphs of history, but also the failures, the tragedies and the humiliations. Facing History believes that students must be trusted to examine history in all of its complexities, including its legacies of prejudice and discrimination, resilience and courage. www.facinghistory.org

Fair Test: The resource center for fair and open testing is an organization works to end the misuses and flaws of standardized testing and to ensure that evaluation of students, teachers and schools is fair, open, valid and educationally beneficial. www.fairtest.org

National Association for Multicultural Education: Is an organization that works on bringing together individuals and groups with an interest in multicultural education from all levels of education, different academic disciplines and from diverse educational institutions and occupations. www.nameorg.org

Resource Center of the Americas: Provides resources that inform, educate and organize to promote human rights, democratic participation, economic justice and cross-cultural understanding in the context of globalization in the Americas.www.americas.org

Teaching for Change: Pre-K-college resources on equity and social justice that provides teachers and parents with the tools to transform schools into socially equitable centers of learning where students become architects of a better future. Teaching for Change is a not-for-profit organization based in Washington, DC. www.teachingforchange.org

Teaching Tolerance: Founded in 1991 by the Southern Poverty Law Center, Teaching Tolerance provides educators with free educational material that promote respect for differences and appreciation of diversity in the classroom and beyond.www.teachingtolerance.org

ABOUT THE AUTHOR

After growing up in generational poverty, leaving school for marriage at 15, having two children, and continuing to cope with poverty, Donna Beegle found herself at 25 with no husband, little education, and no job skills. What followed in 10 short years were self confidence, a GED, an AA, a BA (with honors), a Masters Degree in Communication with a minor in Gender Studies (with honors), and completion of a Doctorate Degree in Educational Leadership.

Donna's inspiring story and work on ending poverty have been featured in newspapers around the nation, on local TV, and on national programs such as PBS. A national public speaker, discussion leader, trainer, and author, Donna Beegle is currently president of Communication Across Barriers, a consulting firm devoted to improving relationships and opportunities across poverty barriers.

Available for:

- Private consulting

- Training

- Curriculum development

- Poverty competency assessments

- Keynote presentations

SEE POVERTY... *Be The Difference!*
